# London

A guide to recent architecture

•••

Samantha Hardingham
Photographs by Keith Collie

# London

12/07/99

Thank you Maria

A guide to recent architecture

● ● ● ellipsis

•••

BRITISH LIBRARY CATALOGUING IN PUBLICATION
A CIP record for this book is available from the British Library

FOURTH EDITION PUBLISHED BY •••ellipsis
2 Rufus Street London N1 6PE
E MAIL ...@ellipsis.co.uk
www http://www.ellipsis.com
SERIES EDITOR Tom Neville
EDITOR Vicky Wilson
SERIES DESIGN Jonathan Moberly

COPYRIGHT © 1999 Ellipsis London Limited
ISBN 1 899858 92 X

FILM PROCESSING METRO IMAGING

PRINTING AND BINDING Hong Kong

•••ellipsis is a trademark of Ellipsis
London Limited

For a copy of the Ellipsis catalogue or
information on special quantity orders
of Ellipsis books please contact
Lindsay Evans
0171–739 3157 or lindsay@ellipsis.co.uk

London: a guide to recent architecture

**Samantha Hardingham 1999**

# Contents

# Introduction

This guide contains descriptions of more than 100 built projects which provide an up-to-date view of London's architectural landscape. The aim of the book is to initiate an architectural tour, pointing out some of the latest building types and techniques along the way. Although projects are discussed individually, it is important to view each one in the larger context of the city. The gaps will be filled by your own observations.

The guide aims to maintain a very current picture, so the content has changed considerably through its four editions within a relatively short space of time. With the imminent arrival of a new millennium the process of architectural evolution has picked up an even brisker pace. Many of the themes outlined in the first edition (produced only five years ago) reflected the events surrounding the building boom of the 1980s and the dominant post-modern style. These concerns have on the whole been superseded by a new wave of development largely encouraged by funds from the National Lottery. However, many of the buildings from that earlier period are still relevant to an understanding of the city's evolution and therefore remain in the guide. Similarly, a brief description of the political climate, then and now, is vital to an understanding of why London looks the way it does today.

Between 1979 and 1997 Britain was in the hands of a Conservative government. In the early 1980s, Prime Minister Margaret Thatcher initiated the deregulation of the public services that form the essential infrastructure of the country. The lifting of state control was supposed to promote competition and, as a result, produce better services. Railways, telecommunications, water, gas, electricity, prisons, prison security and bus services are just some of the public functions that have been wholly or partially privatised. Responsibility has been shifted from local government or national companies to individual private organisations; if these become negligent or insolvent the service deteriorates. In 1986 the Labour-run Greater London Council (GLC) was abolished, and the only voice that could speak for the whole city was replaced by numerous bodies with special areas of interest. The result has been a lack of coordination and a failure to set standards for the fundamental services that make up the city's infrastructure.

The effects on building have been diverse. On the one hand, there has been a dearth of new public housing. As council tenants were encouraged to buy their homes in the 1980s, the government failed to replenish the public-housing stock. On the other hand we simultaneously witnessed a building boom. This was concentrated in the City of London (the financial centre) and the under-developed Docklands where British and North American developers took the opportunity to build vast amounts of office space (providing all the services necessary for computerised trading) and luxury housing to accommodate well-paid employees. Concrete- or steel-framed buildings with granite cladding, sporting pop-classical motifs, were quick to build and provided an instant grandiose façade for any company. Few of these speculative buildings could be listed as examples of distinguished architecture, but they are collectively a social, economic and architectural phenomenon. Today, with a Labour government in power since May 1997, the responsibility for public housing has largely been handed over to independently managed housing associations which provide a limited amount of affordable accommodation. Also, Victorian institutions such as the Peabody Trust (established to provide low-cost housing for the working classes) have recently undergone a resurgence.

Key events that initiated discussions in the early and mid 1980s include the Prince of Wales' debut on the architectural stage at Hampton Court, when he invited the public to participate in a classicism-versus-

**London: a guide to recent architecture**

modernism debate. The Prince seemed certain that living in a Palladian-style cul-de-sac and shopping in a Tudoresque supermarket would preserve the essential qualities of the British Isles while protecting us from the vile threat of modernism. The scheme to redevelop Paternoster Square surrounding St Paul's Cathedral and Lord Palumbo's proposals for the Mappin & Webb building (now No.1 Poultry, see page 236) were both at the centre of such debates. Max Hutchinson, president of the Royal Institute of British Architects (RIBA) at the time, retaliated in a book entitled *The Prince of Wales: Right or Wrong? An Architect Replies* (Faber 1989). A decade later these conversations have filtered through to the regions, enabling our cities to embrace a new generation of ideas.

To some extent a building boom continues, but under the auspices of the National Lottery. The launch of the lottery in 1994 has had a tremendous impact on building in London, enabling a new kind of architectural patronage to emerge. Funds from the scheme have been fed into four departments – the Department of National Heritage, the Arts Council Lottery Fund, the Sports Council and the Millennium Commission – all of which receive proposals for new schemes. Some of these proposals are recently completed (see Sadler's Wells Theatre on page 176 and the Jerwood Space on page 118). Key developments such as the Greenwich Millennium Dome (see page 342) and the new Tate Gallery of Modern Art at Bankside (see page 340), set to open for the new millennium (and their linking by the Jubilee Line Extension, see page 326), will open up a whole new section of London south of the Thames and help to regenerate previously neglected areas such as Southwark and Bermondsey.

Historically the working-class area of the city, much of the East End has been allowed to deteriorate into one of the most poverty-stricken parts of the country, particularly since the decline of industry in Docklands. The concentration of new development at Canary Wharf has reinforced social and economic divides. More recently an attempt has been made to redress the balance and readdress the needs of local communities through the provision of medical centres, schools and youth clubs alongside the migration eastwards of artists and small businesses who cannot afford central London rates. There is still a long way to go. These kinds of projects have provided work for younger architectural practices, who have designed both quick-build schemes and local landmark buildings – often with challenging briefs and budgets – and produced a variety of building types and styles as a direct response to materials technology rather than to trends or images (examples include Penoyre & Prasad's Rushton Street Medical Centre, see page 276, and Branson Coates' new wing at the Geffrye Museum, see page 266).

The imminent opening of the Jubilee Line Extension will unquestionably have the most significant impact on the way London grows and changes demographically, economically, socially and architecturally as we embrace a new millennium. There is also potential in the government's proposals to institute an elected mayor for London. Watch this space …

ACKNOWLEDGEMENTS

An ongoing vote of thanks leaps from one edition to another to all the architects and members of their offices for keeping me up to date with their work, to all those who have written or spoken to me of their enjoyment of the guide, and for my own family's enthusiasm for and scepticism about the subject – these are the things that make writing this book so pleasurable.

SH September 1998

London: a guide to recent architecture

**Using this book**

The guide is divided into ten sections, nine of which define areas of London where there are buildings of interest. Some sections have been stretched to take in exceptional but isolated buildings such as the Crystal Palace concert platform in the deep south. Most of the inner London sections can be covered on foot. The final section covers the extension of the Jubilee underground line and a selection of projects for the millennium. Transport details are listed under each entry. The map coordinates for the standard edition of the *AZ London Street Atlas* are also given after the address to guide you to the precise location of a building.

If you want to read more about any of the buildings, the architects or this particular era I suggest a visit to the library at the Royal Institute of British Architects, Portland Place, London W1 (0171-580 5533; check opening hours and the fee situation before you go). All the periodicals here are well catalogued and there are special files on major projects such as the hugely controversial British Library.

1 **Heathrow to Hammersmith**
2 **Kensington and Chelsea**
3 **Westminster**
4 **South London**
5 **Camden and Islington**
6 **Hampstead**

7 **From the City to Stansted**
8 **Hackney to Stratford**
9 **Docklands**
● **Millennial Sites**
⊖ **Jubilee Line Extension**

# Heathrow to Hammersmith

# Heathrow Airport Visitors' Centre

The Visitors' Centre provides a permanent location for an exhibition that describes how the airport works, promoting the benefits as well as addressing the environmental issues which are raised by its operation. It is both a centre for information (a model of the proposed Terminal 5 project by Richard Rogers is on display) and a new home for the local job centre, serving as a complaints box while at the same time locating the building positively in the community.

The building is made up of two walls which sandwich the main exhibition hall. The north-facing screen wall, clad in steel mesh, extends along the full 100-metre length of the site to separate the exhibition hall from the busy A4 Bath Road. By contrast, the south wall is a thin, transparent box made from a structural steel frame clad in frameless glass. This area accommodates service and access walkways made from galvanised steel grillage (doubling up as solar shading for the interior space). The café on the mezzanine level offers a panoramic view through the south wall of aircraft taking off and landing and acts as an acoustic barrier. The simplicity of structure and clarity of purpose of this small building create a model on which airports themselves should be based.

**Heathrow to Hammersmith**

ADDRESS Newall Road, Hounslow, Middlesex
CLIENT Heathrow Airport Limited
CONTRACT VALUE £3 million
SIZE 18,060 square metres
BY ROAD follow the A4 Great West Road out of Hammersmith. This becomes the Bath Road. Pass the Visitors' Centre on your left, take the next turning left after the Ramada Hotel and follow signs
ACCESS open Tuesday to Friday 10.00–19.00; Saturday 10.00–17.00

**Bennetts Associates 1995**

**Bennetts Associates 1995**

# British Airways Combined Operations Centre/The Compass Centre

The brief was for an aircrew terminal to house all of British Airways' operations staff (12,000 people) and their activities 24 hours a day under one roof. The building also had to have the potential to grow or to be divided for sub-letting. The plan comprises three deep, north/south-facing blocks close to the north runway. Each block is independently serviced by a roof-top plant and connected to the others by full-height glazed links that continue the line of an atrium street running through the centre of all three blocks. This main glazed artery feeds on to cellular office 'neighbourhoods' on either side.

The primary constraints were that sound penetrating the interior had to be controlled to create an ambient working environment, height was limited to three storeys, and the visibility of the building's mass on the air-traffic controllers' radar screens had to be minimised. So materials that are not highly reflective to radar energy had to be chosen (metal is very reflective, carbon foams are very absorbent but prohibitively expensive, wet surfaces are more reflective than dry ones, a fragmented surface with soft corners diffuses reflection more than a smooth one with sharp corners, and so on), making this the first building in Britain to be designed for radar transparency.

These restrictions have manifested themselves primarily in the design of the envelope. The building is sited at an angle to and set back from the boundary and surrounded by a car park and landscaping (trees and bushes are good noise and radar refractors). The frame is concrete rather than steel. An extensive use of glass combined with the convex curtain-walled façades and external horizontal solar shading help to minimise radar reflections, cut out internal light reflection and deflect noise. Aluminium mullions formed in aerofoil profiles and aluminium cladding

**Nicholas Grimshaw & Partners 1993**

**Heathrow to Hammersmith**

**Nicholas Grimshaw & Partners 1993**

panels formed in a convex shape to produce a pillowed surface further reduce the potential of interference with radar. The horizontally faceted curtain walls combined with the blue-fritted louvred sunshades reflect radar to the ground and cut out direct sunlight. External lighting has been incorporated into the spandrel panels of the curtain walling so the building is not visible from the air at night. The lighting, combined with a blue-fritted outer pane and solid inner pane, produces a deep glow at night and a voluminous cobalt blue building by day, making this the most visible invisible building in London.

Some of the architects' own preoccupations emerge. The convex façades are reminiscent of the *Western Morning News* offices in Dorset, though a lack of any shading device there led to uncomfortable levels of heat absorption and glare – internal blinds were added later.

ADDRESS Heathrow Airport, located between the Bath Road (A4) and the airport's Northern Perimeter Road
CLIENT Heathrow Airport Limited (Lynton plc)
STRUCTURAL ENGINEER YRM Anthony Hunt Associates
FIT-OUT Aukett Associates
CONTRACT VALUE £17 million (shell and core)
SIZE 22,000 square metres
TUBE Heathrow – Piccadilly Line
ACCESS none

**Nicholas Grimshaw & Partners 1993**

**Heathrow to Hammersmith**

Nicholas Grimshaw & Partners 1993

# Stockley Park

Forty minutes' drive from central London, 20 minutes to the M25 and the rest of the UK, and five minutes by taxi to Heathrow Airport and the rest of the world. In 1984 Stuart Lipton of Stanhope Properties plc led a masterplan to clear up this 100-hectare site, which had been used as a dump for metropolitan rubbish since 1916, and transform it into a new breed of business park. After research into the toxicity of the soil, 3.5 million cubic metres of rubbish were ceremoniously moved north to create a 'naturally' contoured landscape.

Lipton made sure that no expense was spared in making this the only place large international companies would want for their UK headquarters. Land reclamation was carried out by a firm from the Netherlands, trees were brought in from Belgium, geese from Hawaii, Sir Norman Foster, Ian Ritchie, Troughton McAslan, Sir Richard Rogers, Eric Parry, Skidmore, Owings & Merrill, Inc., and Geoffrey Darke were commissioned to design buildings (all variations on the theme of a shell-and-core, two- or three-storey, steel-framed construction), and the Prince of Wales performed the opening ceremony. The idea was to create a high-quality environment that could service nearby towns as well as the business community – social facilities include a nursery, health club, golf course, bars and restaurants and a bus service linked to local schools. All that is needed to complete the picture is a uniform for all employees – a Star Trek outfit would be more appropriate here than a pin-stripe suit.

Arup Associates as masterplanners have designed more than 12 buildings on the site, providing adaptable space for a range of high-technology industries. They are designed as a series of pavilions with landscaped gardens immediately surrounding each one. In 1990 a total of 140,000 square metres of space was constructed.

The most recent addition is No.3 The Square, a 790-square-metre

**Arup Associates 1984–**

**Arup Associates 1984–**

office building also designed by Arup Associates. Here a new type of building has been developed with an emphasis on reduced running costs, openable windows, warm, natural materials and offices with views. The result turns the 1980s idea of an atrium inside out: a cruciform plan is wrapped in a square glass envelope forming four corner conservatories so office floors within a maple-veneer-clad cruciform block become outward looking and have windows opening on to naturally ventilated conservatory areas. Only the cruciform internal floorplate is considered for planning permission and not the surrounding atria spaces because these have no specific social function.

Other pavilions constructed to date include:

A1.1, A1.2, A1.3, A2.1, A2.2, A2.3, A3.1, A3.2, B1 – Arup Associates
B2 (Apple Computers) – Troughton McAslan
B3 (BP) – Foster Associates
B4 (Apple Computers Phase II) – Troughton McAslan
B5 and B7 – Arup Associates
B6 – Geoffrey Darke
B8 – Ian Ritchie Architects
B9, B10 and B11 – Skidmore, Owings & Merrill, Inc.
B12 – Eric Parry Associates
Arena Building (leisure complex) – Arup Associates

ADDRESS Stockley Park, Heathrow, Middlesex
ENGINEER Ove Arup & Partners
LANDSCAPE DESIGN Bernard Ede and Charles Funke
BY ROAD leave M4 at junction 4, on to A408 (Stockley Road). Stockley Park is approximately 1.5 kilometres north
ACCESS the business park is open

**Arup Associates 1984–**

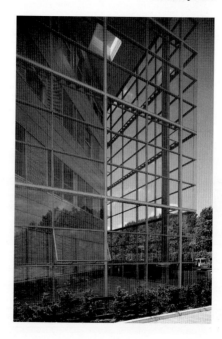

**Arup Associates 1984–**

# The London Ark

As you cruise on to the Hammersmith flyover, the Ark immediately communicates that this is not just any office block. The building readdresses the traditional form of the centrally governed business by creating a working community in which different companies can develop their own identity and contribute to the character of the common social environment contained within the central atrium – 'like a town under a roof'.

A significant step towards an ecologically-sound office building, the Ark challenges the conventions of the building services which are often the cause of sick building syndrome. The air conditioning, for example, fixed to the ceiling, circulates a fresh-air supply through diffusers and across water-cooler batteries (set at 14°C to prevent condensation). The stale air is discharged through ventilators in the timber-lined atrium roof. Heating is a ceiling-mounted radiant system, using low-pressure hot water from a gas-fired boiler plant. Triple glazing reduces heat loss as well as shutting out traffic noise from the flyover. The 15,000 square metres of tiered, open-plan office space are flooded with natural light from the core. Information and air should both flow freely around the building.

Bands of copper cladding, attached to the steel frame, appear to be protecting the delicate interior environment from the harsh exterior one, like a coat of armour. Although originally unpleasantly and overpoweringly brown, in time the copper will turn green. It is unfortunate that the clumsy brick supports will not undergo a similar, seemingly biological, transformation.

Ecologically sound inside maybe, but residents living in streets directly behind the Ark are suffering the effects of noise from nearby underground trains rebounding off the curved side of the building and landing in their back gardens. Erskine's response is to build a section of park over the exposed train lines, thereby deadening the noise and providing a new

**Ralph Erskine 1991**

**Ralph Erskine 1991**

**Heathrow to Hammersmith**

public space. We shall have to wait and see whether or not this actually materialises.

When designed it was hoped that the Ark would set a precedent for the development of environments for living and working – not just existing in – and that this would give rise to new building types and the redefinition of old ones. Now, in the late 1990s, there is clear evidence to suggest that the principles it set out are being more widely adopted. The use of natural materials, the evolution of a more organic plan and making maximum use of daylight all appear in some form or other in building types from galleries (see the Geffrye Museum, page 266) through medical centres (see the Rushton Street Medical Centre, page 276) to office blocks (see No.3 The Square at Stockley Park, page 20).

ADDRESS Talgarth Road, London W6 [5F 75]
CLIENT Ake Larson and Pronator
ASSOCIATED ARCHITECTS Lennart Bergstrom Architects/Rock Townsend Architects
PROJECT VALUE £33.5 million
TUBE Hammersmith – District, Hammersmith & City, Piccadilly Lines
ACCESS try telephoning Architectural Tours (0181-341 1371) for an appointment

**Ralph Erskine 1991**

**Ralph Erskine 1991**

Heathrow to Hammersmith

# Thames Reach Housing and Thames Wharf Studios

This was once a Duckham's Oil depot, housed in two Edwardian brick warehouses with a 1950s concrete block slung on the eastern end of the site. Rogers chose the 1950s block for his own offices. The glass and steel-work were reconstructed but the essence of the building remains the same – that is, the huge floor plates and the spectacular view across the river. There are windows on three sides of the building with the service core in the centre. The distinctive glass barrel-vaulted roof is a later addition, designed by Lifschutz Davidson Design.

One of the warehouses has been converted into workshop-type studio spaces which are occupied mainly by designers and craftsmen. The River Café is on the ground floor, opening on to a garden terrace on the river-front. The warehouse to the west has been turned into apartments. All the original load-bearing brick and blockwork remain the same – not an approach instantly associated with Rogers' previous high-tech record – but the white-painted steel balconies, balustrades and walkways strapped on to each block are undoubtedly his.

The client played a prominent role in the design of the housing block, having a clear idea of the demands of the up-market occupants being targeted. The design of the dull interiors was contracted out to a more conventional interior designer. However, the river frontage is spectacular, with glazed curtain-wall façades facing south-west. Venetian blinds and natural through ventilation combat solar-heat gain. The glass-brick tower that projects upwards from one of the blocks is part of John Young's private apartment.

Rogers' theme is the creation of a community with shared public facilities and open-plan living and working spaces. His office is a community in its own right with the café and crèche facilities for its employees. The

**Richard Rogers Partnership/Lifschutz Davidson Design 1984–1987**

**Richard Rogers Partnership/Lifschutz Davidson Design 1984–1987**

lettable studio space, occupied by design-oriented trades and industries, helps to fuel the working community while the opening up of another section of the riverside walk from Hammersmith to Putney Bridges adds to the public domain. The exercise here is one in urbanism rather than architectonics.

ADDRESS Rainville Road, London W6 [6E 74]
CLIENTS Housing: Croudace Construction; Studios: Marco Goldschied, Richard Rogers, John Young; Offices: H H Peggs; River Café: Richard and Ruth Rogers
STRUCTURAL ENGINEER Ove Arup & Partners/Hay Barry & Partners
CONTRACT VALUE £1034 per square metre
TUBE Hammersmith – District, Hammersmith & City, Piccadilly Lines
ACCESS limited

**Richard Rogers Partnership/Lifschutz Davidson Design 1984–1987**

**Heathrow to Hammersmith**

**Richard Rogers Partnership/Lifschutz Davidson Design 1984–1987**

**Richmond Riverside**

The site of this royally approved scheme is bound by the River Thames to the south, Hill Street to the north, Bridge Street to the east and the rest of Richmond village stretching out to the west. The brief was to provide 9900 square metres of office space, two restaurants, 28 flats and parking space for 135 cars. All this is disguised behind a Hollywood vision of old London town; convincing, but for the distinct lack of festive cheer about the place. Some of the original buildings still exist on the site, although they are hard to pick out … at first glance.

Face the scheme from across the river. On the left is a square block of two storeys, with arched windows and a roof surmounted by a cupola (the significance of this detail will become apparent in a moment). It is decorated with Doric and Ionic columns, drawing its jumble of references directly from Palladian villas, but here is used as a restaurant. Behind this, running adjacent to the river, is the town hall (called 'The Castle'), built in 1873 by W J Ancell. Only the façade remains, looking like the leftovers of a Regency square. Next to it is the old town hall, now a public library, with a new French mansard roof (presumably added to increase floor space). Next along is the entirely new Hotham House, built in a patchy Georgian style which is given away by its genuine next-door neighbour, Heron House, built in 1716. Heron House has been fully restored and provides access through an archway into the new central square. The square is full of stucco buildings which are trying hard to pass themselves off as 100- to 200-year-olds when really they have barely reached their tenth birthday. The row is terminated by the prettier Italianate Tower House, built in 1856 by Laxton. The Hill Street and Bridge Street façades are lined with arcades, each block defined by a different Order.

All the new structures are built of load-bearing brick and lime mortar with reinforced-concrete slab floors and Welsh-slate roofs. The appro-

**Erith & Terry 1988**

**Erith & Terry 1988**

priate accoutrements are on the outside but functions have changed. Chimneys sitting on party walls and decorative cupolas (here's the trick) now become essential as disguises for modern air vents and ducting. On entering any of the buildings you realise the full extent of the exercise in deception when you see the bog-standard 1960s-style office interiors jammed between the neo-Georgian/Palladian/gothic-Venetian façades. Raised floors and suspended ceilings cut through the full height of the windows, obtrusive both inside and out. The architect, Quinlan Terry, is reported to be equally disappointed with the interiors, but surely such a vital detail could have been accommodated within a less dogmatic plan.

Terry's ideal is 'to return to the letter and spirit of the Classical world, a world that is characterised by order'. The nature of Classicism is its truth and purity of form; the nature of the Classical Orders is that they are structural rather than ornamental: inside and outside were one and the same thing. Modernism (Mr Terry has called the movement 'a sign of the fall from grace') has more in common with the style and nature of Classicism than this architect is prepared to admit. Richmond Riverside is the scheme that architects love to hate but it seems to go down well with the local residents.

ADDRESS Richmond, Surrey [2J 89]
CLIENT Haslemere Estates
CONTRACT VALUE £20 million
TUBE Richmond – District Line
BR Richmond
ACCESS open

**Heathrow to Hammersmith**

**Erith & Terry 1988**

**Erith & Terry 1988**

# Shri Swaminarayan Mandir, Neasden

Caught in the sprawling web of the A404, A406 (commonly known as the North Circular) and A407 is an architectural jewel unlike any other in this guide. The Mandir (the Hindu word for temple) and Haveli (courtyard house – the Cultural Complex) are the first to be built outside the Indian subcontinent. Extensive research was carried out including a study tour of north-west India (where the Aryan people entered India from Persia as early as 5000 BC to form the Vedic civilisation, the precursor of Hinduism). The design process involved close collaboration between the architects, engineers and members of the Swaminarayan Hindu Mission to take account of the British weather and statutory building requirements alongside the wishes of the Mission to have a mandir true to the designs laid down in the ancient architectural texts, the *Shilpashastras*. However, the existing building is not a replica of any other and its design brought together strands of several ancient architectural styles and methods.

Climate and pollution ruled out the use of red sandstone as the primary building material for the Mandir itself, and Vedic principles ban the use of ferrous materials. Vedic tradition was translated into working drawings to satisfy local authorities and the solution of an inner mandir of marble with a weatherproof outer enclosure of carved limestone was arrived at. The adjacent Haveli – comprising living accommodation for the attendant Sadhus, an administration area and a community meeting place – was developed from the study of the domestic architectural traditions of north-west India. The carved timber (Burmese teak and English oak), adopted from the carved temples of Gujarat, has not been recreated in India or anywhere else in the last 100 years.

The Mandir design incorporates a 7-metre-diameter central mandapa (dome) surrounded by seven conical shikhars (spires) which house the

**Chandrakant B Sompura/Triad Architects Planners 1995**

Chandrakant B Sompura/Triad Architects Planners 1995

murtis (deities) and provide places beneath for contemplation. Twelve hundred tons of Carrara marble and 3000 tons of Vrataza Bulgarian limestone were shipped to Kandal in Gujarat where 1000 Indian stonemasons hand-carved the stone before shipping it back to the UK. An additional 920 tons of Ambaji marble were carved in Rajasthan in a specially created workshop near the quarry. Specialist stonemasons and craftsmen were flown to the UK from India to supervise the construction. The intention was to make the structure appear as an organic whole when in fact it was made in finely carved sections. The internal structure is a vast jigsaw-puzzle assembly of marble dowels and light cement.

In India a mandir would be partially open to the elements to provide natural ventilation. In west London underfloor heating and double glazing at ground-floor level are the order of the day, leaving the veil of intricate traceried limestone surrounding the building to convey a sense of airy authenticity. A visit to the Mandir and Haveli is one of the more surprising, profoundly unusual and – yes – truly religious experiences to be had in London. Its appearance on the city's architectural map indicates how building styles and techniques are becoming more global and more adaptable as cultural demands become increasingly specific.

ADDRESS 105/115 Brentfield Road, London NW10 [6K 41]
CLIENT Swaminarayan Hindu Mission
STRUCTURAL ENGINEER Austin Trueman
CONTRACT VALUE £25 million
SIZE 10,000 square metres/3.85-hectare site
TUBE Neasden – Jubilee Line
ACCESS open 09.00–12.00 and 16.00–18.00; remove shoes in the foyer area of the Haveli and observe silence in the Mandir

**Chandrakant B Sompura/Triad Architects Planners 1995**

**Heathrow to Hammersmith**

**Chandrakant B Sompura/Triad Architects Planners 1995**

# Kensington and Chelsea

# Thames Water Ring Main Tower

A student competition was held for a structure that would hide a surge pipe in the middle of the Shepherd's Bush roundabout and at the same time celebrate the vast £250 million ring-main project which now embraces central London. The winning entry was designed by students from the Royal College of Art, who created this 15-metre-high barometer. The round tower is made of steel and glass (with the service ladder in the middle) and is animated by coloured water contained within the curved glass walls. This spirals its way up and down the tower to indicate the climatic extremes.

The adjacent classical shed is not related in any way to the winning design and is best ignored.

**Kensington and Chelsea**

ADDRESS Shepherd's Bush roundabout, London W12 [F2 75]
CLIENT Thames Water
CONSULTANT ARCHITECT Alan Brooks Associates
STRUCTURAL ENGINEER Neil Thomas
TUBE Shepherd's Bush – Central, Hammersmith & City Lines

**Damien O'Sullivan/Tania Doufa 1994**

**Kensington and Chelsea**

**Damien O'Sullivan/Tania Doufa 1994**

# Westbourne Grove Public Lavatories

The project encompasses the whole of the triangular traffic island to incorporate landscape design as well as the design of the building itself. CZWG's unmistakeable approach comes into its own in this small but provocative urban folly. The three-sided plan has grown out of the shape of the site: the wide end accommodates the lavatories and attendant's kiosk and the pointed end of the triangle is a florist's kiosk. The pale aquamarine glazed-brick walls sit on the pavement like a slice of delectable gateau, topped by a delicate glazed canopy roof with the clock stuck on the corner like a glacé cherry. Each feature is exploited to the full, even down to the stylised supergraphics on the lavatory doors to distinguish the GENTS from the LADIES.

There is no doubt that it is an improvement on its predecessors. It is unusually generous with space when so often minimum standard dimensions are applied for a facility of this type. A bold move by the local residents (the Pembridge Association actually promoted the idea of commissioning CZWG) to change the face of their neighbourhood.

ADDRESS junction of Colville Road and Westbourne Grove, London W11 [6H 59]
CLIENT The Royal Borough of Kensington and Chelsea Council Offices
STRUCTURAL ENGINEER Dewhurst Macfarlane & Partners
CONTRACT VALUE £190,000
SIZE site 700 square metres, building 60 square metres
TUBE Notting Hill Gate – Central, Circle, District Lines; Westbourne Grove – Hammersmith & City Line (both require a 5-minute walk to reach the site)
ACCESS open

Kensington and Chelsea

**CZWG Architects 1993**

**CZWG Architects 1993**

# Wild At Heart

This is the second home of the wildly successful flower stall which trades off the back of CZWG's public WCs (see page 44) around the corner in Westbourne Grove. The project may well be a demonstration of a future-system for applying a new shop front to an old building without having to fudge any joins, but the design inside is simply an impulsive response to the current fashion, with a seamless white interior providing a stark contrast with (in this case) a minimal display of flowers. The front is a single piece of glass bolted directly on top of the old frontage. An amorphous-shaped frame is sand-blasted into the surface, obscuring the overlap and creating an equally seamless window opening.

As Future Systems build more of their projects it is becoming increasingly apparent that the smooth organic forms that appear on their drawings are executed in a peculiarly mechanical manner – as if the materials technology has not yet been created to achieve the required effect. Here the cast-aluminium front steps, which perhaps in conception poured out of the shop front and on to the pavement, are in reality nothing more than an obstruction in the freeway – an accident waiting to happen to some unsuspecting passer-by doing a spot of harmless window shopping but ending up falling into the store. It's one way of luring in customers, I suppose.

ADDRESS 49a Ledbury Road, London W11 [6H 59]
CLIENT Nikki Tibbles and Oliver Backhouse
STRUCTURAL ENGINEER Ove Arup & Partners
TUBE Bayswater – Circle, District Lines; Notting Hill Gate – Central, Circle, District Lines; Royal Oak – Hammersmith & City Line
ACCESS during shop-opening hours

**Ecology Gallery**
**Natural History Museum**

The gallery accommodates the ecology exhibit in a chasm of Optiwhite glass, illuminated with coloured lights to create the illusion of fire, water and a sheer glacial wall. Clear strips are cut into the walls, like rubbing the frost off windows, to reveal exhibits and parts of the existing building. Look out for literary quotes etched into the glass. Ribbed bellies of bridges traverse the corridor above your head to connect the different themes exhibited upstairs. Each bridge floor is made from a different material, evoking different aspects of the earth and its elements. These platforms allow you to pause and float in the space, to absorb your surroundings before you are drawn into the walls again to walk inside a leaf or be shovelled up by a giant digger.

Ritchie's environment is both interactive and reflective. Although some of the detailing is a bit flimsy the overall effect is informative and convincing.

ADDRESS Cromwell Road, London SW7 [4K 75]
CLIENT Natural History Museum
STRUCTURAL ENGINEER Ove Arup & Partners
CONTRACT VALUE £2 million
SIZE 3000 square metres
TUBE South Kensington – Circle, District, Piccadilly Lines
ACCESS open 10.00–17.50 daily

**Ian Ritchie Architects 1991**

Kensington and Chelsea

**Ian Ritchie Architects 1991**

# Dinosaur Gallery
**Natural History Museum**

This is a triumph of modernisation and preservation over mundane conservation. A new 84-metre raised walkway runs the full length of the Dinosaur Gallery in Alfred Waterhouse's elaborate Victorian neo-gothic palace of natural science. The tensegrity structure's function is three-fold. First, in order to enhance the existing structure it holds services that illuminate the Victorian carvings of fish and animals on columns, treading lightly around these parts that previously went unnoticed. Second, it provides new circulation, views of the exhibits on the ground and opportunities for close inspection of the old details. Third, it forms a framework from which to hang dinosaur skeletons (a slight give in the cables causes them to twitch ominously).

Unfortunately, Imagination's temporary exhibition displays do not correspond to possible views from the mezzanine. This lack of coherence should be rectified, but in the meantime you can enjoy the primary structure and its obvious spiny qualities.

**Kensington and Chelsea**

ADDRESS Cromwell Road, London SW7 [4K 75]
CLIENT Natural History Museum
STRUCTURAL ENGINEER Ove Arup & Partners
TUBE South Kensington – Circle, District, Piccadilly Lines
ACCESS open 10.00–17.50 daily

**Herron Associates @ Imagination 1992**

**Herron Associates @ Imagination 1992**

# Wonders Exhibition
## Natural History Museum

A modest work from an office which has received significant commissions in Germany and Tokyo. The museum has made an enlightened choice of architect in the past to regenerate interest. In this case, David Chipperfield was commissioned to redesign reception and admissions furniture and a display system for the permanent Wonders Exhibition in the bays of the main hall. The reception furniture has a characteristically Japanese horizontality: wooden slatted bases and sand-blasted glass screens which do not try to challenge the magnificence of the dinosaur skeleton in its grand gothic abode (nor do they expose a new vision of the space as has Herron's intervention in the Dinosaur Gallery, see page 50).

The two main issues for the exhibition design to address were how to mediate between the monumental scale of the existing space and the small objects to be displayed, and how to accommodate the varying scale of the exhibits themselves in a unified way. Located in each bay is a uniform 4 x 4-metre primed-steel wall. Each one has been customised to accommodate different objects by cutting out niches or adding shelves and plinths. The walls conceal all necessary lighting and monitor equipment, leaving a blank surface to show off the objects. Continuity is maintained between all the elements with the uniform shape and details in cast bronze, as found throughout the rest of the museum.

ADDRESS Cromwell Road, London SW7 [4K 75]
CLIENT Natural History Museum
TUBE South Kensington – Circle, District, Piccadilly Lines
ACCESS open 10.00–17.50 daily

**David Chipperfield Architects 1993**

Kensington and Chelsea

**David Chipperfield Architects 1993**

# The Basement

### Science Museum

Following their industrial-chic design for the Hacienda nightclub in Manchester (1982), BKD won a limited competition to make 'a Hacienda for children' at the Science Museum – a unique opportunity to de-institutionalise an institution and devise a plan that would open a child's imagination to the wonders of science. The masterplan was for an entirely new facility for younger children and school parties comprising a large communal area including the Terrace, the Arcade, the Information Wall and Eat Drink Shop; the Lift Exchange (designed by John Lyall Architects); the Girls and Boys lavatory block; the Spare Room; Switch (a visible plant room); and two playroom/galleries called the Garden (by Casson Mann) and Things (by Giles Cernazandotti).

There are three ways of entering the Basement: by stairs from the ground-floor galleries; by lift; or via a separate new entrance on Imperial College Road (also part of the masterplan). This last is used primarily by school parties and from here children can stash their bags in lockers and run down a long, wide corridor into the main space (like a players' tunnel opening on to a football pitch). The main space is conceived as a town square where groups can congregate on the low, deep steps of the Terrace to have their lunch, watch a performance or demonstration (the museum organises an ongoing programme of short educational events throughout the day) or look across to the individual gallery rooms. The Arcade (daylit from above) runs the length of the space behind the Terrace, providing disabled access to the back of the Terrace and therefore unhindered access to the entire plan (instead of confining all disabled visitors to designated zones, as is the norm in public facilities).

Key to the success of the project is BKD's ability to integrate thoroughly strong colour, tactile materials and a sense of humour into all the facilities rather than applying these qualities as an afterthought to a municipal

**Ben Kelly Design 1995**

**Ben Kelly Design 1995**

shell. Every element has been considered as a way of engaging a child in a given activity: from the abstract outlines of low-tech waste products embedded in the lino floor (designed in collaboration with artist Tim Head) to the colour-coded sections of the building's structure that have been cut away to create the present interior space (see the I-beams in the Arcade) and the graded heights of the urinals and sinks in the lavatory block. The smooth, richly coloured glaze of the wall tiles and hardwearing terrazzo steps with recycled plastic seats are both unaggressive and indestructable (the museum estimates that during termtime 2500 children visit the Basement each day). This means parents and teachers need worry less about their frustrated children pressing crisps and chocolate into the carpet and more about how they are going to extract them at closing time from experimenting with sound and light in the Garden.

This is an exercise not in dumbing-down but in switching on. Highly recommended for children of all ages.

ADDRESS Exhibition Road, London SW7 [2B 76]
CLIENT Science Museum
STRUCTURAL ENGINEER Dewhurst Macfarlane & Partners
SIZE 2124 square metres
TUBE South Kensington – Circle, District, Piccadilly Lines
ACCESS open 10.00–17.50 daily

**Kensington and Chelsea**

**Ben Kelly Design 1995**

Kensington and Chelsea

**Ben Kelly Design 1995**

# Suspension Bridge
## Challenge of Materials Gallery, Science Museum

This is one of the smaller projects from this rapidly expanding practice, but is no less sophisticated for that. The overall scheme for the new Challenge of Materials Gallery reinstates the two-storey atrium (previously closed off) of the first main gallery encountered by visitors on their arrival. New displays have been created (with exhibition designer Jasper Jacobs Associates) in the north and south mezzanine gallery spaces connected at first-floor level by the centrepiece of the project – an elegant 12-metre-long suspension bridge.

The purpose of the bridge is to inform visitors about modern materials, using interactive means. And what could keep you on your interactive toes more effectively than a walk across a bridge designed to the edge of technological feasibility? The floor is made of laminated-glass sections, suspended by four cobwebs of stainless-steel wires each measuring less than 1 millimetre in diameter, which, like their natural counterparts, disappear under certain lighting conditions. The wires are attached to stress gauges connected to a fibre-optic display and synthesiser, so as you cross the bridge sound effects (provided by Ron Geesin) and light conditions change according to the variation in the load.

Take a look from the bridge across to the gravity-defying steel-framed family house, suspended from the ceiling on equally fine wires.

ADDRESS Exhibition Road, London SW7 [2B 76]
CLIENT Science Museum
STRUCTURAL ENGINEER Whitby & Bird
CONTRACT VALUE partly subsidised by the steel industry
TUBE South Kensington – Circle, District, Piccadilly Lines
ACCESS open 10.00–17.50 daily

**Chris Wilkinson Architects 1998**

Kensington and Chelsea

Kensington and Chelsea

**Chris Wilkinson Architects 1998**

**Serpentine Gallery**

Originally designed on a symmetrical Palladian plan as the Serpentine Tea Pavilion (1934) by the chief architect to H M Office of Works, J Grey West OBE, the building has been a public gallery since 1970 and more recently has become one of the first projects in London to be completed with the aid of lottery funding. The ambitions of the gallery's trustees (to continue to house the work of contemporary artists and to obtain government indemnity to accommodate any work from the national collection) could not be achieved in a building with no adequate storage and security, no means of temperature and humidity control and a leaking roof.

The architects were commissioned (presumably on the basis that the practice prides itself on discreet, practical interventions) to improve the gallery's organisation and efficiency within the existing ground plan – as the building is Grade II listed and owned by the Royal Parks, any visible additions had to be in character with the existing fabric. External repairs were carried out using Westmoreland slate and bricks from the original supplier. (I have not spotted any yet, but I am told that some of the bricks have a smooth glazed finish where the sand has turned to glass in the firing process.) The roof terrace is still strictly out of bounds because the budget could not stretch to strengthening it for public use. Structurally, the most significant change is the excavation of a new basement to house a plant room, stores and a workshop. A concrete slab was cast on the ground floor and then dug out from beneath.

The gallery spaces have been maintained in profile but the route has been formalised. However, the quality of the spaces has been altered by the introduction of new skylights with external automatic sunscreen blinds, a new internal artifical-lighting system, air-conditioning, security shutters embedded in the ceilings and a continuous surface of granolithic tiles on the floor.

**John Miller & Partners 1997**

**John Miller & Partners 1997**

Formerly visitors could wander casually from the park into the gallery through tall French doors on the north and east sides. Now the entrance has been consolidated with the bookshop, lavatories and foyer. Offices are on the first floor above the entrance and extend over the South Gallery. An education room occupies the old north entrance, sealing off this side of the building. Landscaping of the area surrounding the gallery was executed in close collaboration with the Royal Parks landscape architect Hal Moggridge. The entrance forecourt incorporates the first permanent Ian Hamilton Finlay installation in London.

Although the new scheme has provided more appropriate accommodation for the offices and bookshop, the addition of a formal entrance and an education room (isn't the gallery itself an education room?) has compromised the relaxed qualities of the original pavilion. The combination of the necklace of spots beneath the dome and the disc to disguise and support fluorescent and track lighting is an indelicate feature. The new gallery does not prohibit visitors by charging an admission fee, but the process of formalisation has taken away the sense of discovery felt every time one stumbled into the building, whether one knew it was a gallery or not.

ADDRESS Kensington Gardens, Hyde Park, London W2 [2B 76]
CLIENT Trustees of the Serpentine Gallery
STRUCTURAL ENGINEER WSP Consulting Engineers
CONTRACT VALUE £2.8 million
SIZE 1061 square metres (ground and first floor)
TUBE South Kensington – Circle, District, Piccadilly Lines
ACCESS open 10.00–18.00 daily

**John Miller & Partners 1997**

# Michelin House

Michelin House is the Grade II-listed original British headquarters of the Michelin Tyre Company. It has been restored and converted to accommodate the offices of the Paul Hamlyn Publishing Group, the Conran Shop and Oyster Bar and the Bibendum Restaurant.

The original construction is a reinforced-concrete frame, the first of its kind in England, designed by an untrained architect. Sixty steel columns have been threaded through the existing floors to support a new fourth floor without obstructing the main shop at ground level – a proposal of such complexity that it took 1300 separate drawings to detail it. Another new feature is the glazed wall on the Sloane Avenue façade which encloses the old loading bay, providing more shop space.

Original features have been lovingly restored, from the glass cupolas on each side of the Brompton Road entrance and the stained-glass window of Bibendum to the tiles that run around what was the tyre-fitting bay and is now the stage for the lobster-seller. Damaged tiles were patched with pigmented resin. It is fashionable to peruse the contents of the shop on Saturday mornings, buy an esoteric coal bucket from Bangalore, spot a design guru slurping oysters and then roam around the rest of Brompton Cross identifying other architect-designed shops.

ADDRESS Brompton Road, London SW3 [4C 76]
CLIENTS Paul Hamlyn, Sir Terence Conran
STRUCTURAL ENGINEER YRM Anthony Hunt Associates
CONTRACT VALUE £9 million
SIZE 36,500 square metres total
TUBE South Kensington – Circle, District, Piccadilly Lines
ACCESS open

**Conran Roche (after François Espinasse, 1911) 1986–1987**

**Conran Roche (after François Espinasse, 1911) 1986–1987**

# Chelsea and Westminster Hospital

Following the closure of Westminster Hospital in Horseferry Road, this hospital embodies a government scheme to amalgamate many of London's hospitals, providing fewer beds for complex cases and leaving the rest to attend 'Super Health Centres' which I'm afraid don't actually exist yet (well, not in every community). Chelsea and Westminster Hospital provides 666 beds, clinical, research and teaching facilities, on-site accommodation for approximately 300 staff and medical students, a mental-health unit for 80 patients and facilities for out-patients. It was commissioned and completed in a record 42 months.

With the exception of the rather heavy canopy designed by the engineers Atelier One, the brick and glass warehouse-look, five-storey front elevation (suggesting wide-span floors reaching from front to back) gives you no indication of what lies behind. The interior design focuses on a naturally ventilated central atrium, rising to seven storeys. It is covered by a pneumatic ETFE (ethylene tetra-fluorothylene) roof membrane, the largest expanse ever used to roof an atrium. The triple-layer foil membrane forms highly insulated cushions kept inflated by a constant stream of air fed through the extruded aluminium framework. The ground-floor mall creates a semi-outdoor environment, providing seating/café areas, a pharmacy, crèche, hospital chapel and access to all departments in the building via three lift cores. The chapel is an independent structure within the atrium, emphasising the street-like quality of the space. Its stained-glass windows were transferred from the old Westminster Hospital.

Three ante-atria on each side of the central space form light wells at the centre of the wards, and administrative offices run around the perimeter of the building. The walls are lined with horizontal fins called Helmholtz resonators to absorb frequencies of sound which might build up

**Sheppard Robson Architects 1993**

**Kensington and Chelsea**

**Sheppard Robson Architects 1993**

throughout the vast internal spaces. The huge fins at the bottom of each well are part of the natural-ventilation system: open in the summer, they draw cool air in from the outside. Heat generated from the perimeter rooms is used to warm the atrium in winter. At the rear of the building, housed in a two-storey basement, there is a combined heat and power plant which generates electricity for the hospital; excess power is sold on to the London Electricity Board, feeding into the city's grid. Visual and physical links between all areas of the hospital have been created with uncovered walkways which traverse the central atrium.

The hospital has pioneered an impressive arts programme, with commissioned works by Allen Jones (*Acrobatic Dancer* – see more of Jones' work at the Hilton Hotel, Terminal 4, Heathrow), textiles by Sian Tucker, murals by Melvyn Chantrey, tapestry by Mary Fogg and a hanging by Patrick Heron. To my surprise the building did not have the usual disinfectant/boiled-food aroma that impregnates so many hospitals – 'catering' has wisely been located beyond the rear of the atrium. Before you get that far down the 116-metre-long space your breath has already been taken away by the innumerable innovative features.

ADDRESS Fulham Road, London SW6 [2G 91]
CLIENT Riverside Health Authority
CONTRACT VALUE £177 million
SIZE 111,500 square metres
BUS 14, 211 to Fulham Road
ACCESS to the central atrium

**Kensington and Chelsea**

**Sheppard Robson Architects 1993**

**Sheppard Robson Architects 1993**

# Riverside Offices and Apartments

A simple concrete and glass structure located on an industrial site between Albert Bridge and Battersea Bridge with a spectacular riverside frontage; an entire working, living and relaxing environment has been created, looking its best when illuminated at night.

From the crumbling back-street approach one is transported into a crisp white space. At the top of a grand flight of stone steps the receptionist sits behind a Nomos table and employees seated on Foster barstools take coffee at the bar overlooking the elegant reception/gallery space, the main office and the river beyond.

Huge 'dinosaur' tables stretch out across the vast, light-filled studio floor. Each workstation accommodates a whole project team, storage for their drawings and a Totem (a vertical post designed by Foster to house electricity, computer and telephone sockets). Extra meeting tables, Eames wire chairs and project models are displayed along the glazed river frontage. On the south side a mezzanine floor houses an audio-visual room, with the slide and technical libraries above and a sound-proofed machine workshop and computer rooms below.

The upper floors are occupied by glass-fronted luxury apartments with the architect's own home atop the rigorously Foster-designed empire.

ADDRESS 22 Hester Road, London SW11 [7C 76]
CLIENT Petmoor Developments
STRUCTURAL ENGINEER Ove Arup & Partners
SITE AREA 4000 square metres
BUILDING AREA 2000 square metres
BUS 19, 45A, 49, 249, 349 to the south side of Battersea Bridge
ACCESS none

**Foster Associates 1990**

**Foster Associates 1990**

# Westminster

# Clore Gallery
## Tate Gallery

In 1851, 290 oil paintings and 20,000 works on paper by J M W Turner were left to the nation. The collection was dispersed following flooding in the Tate and war damage, and as a result much of the work was stored in the Print Room of the British Museum. The daughter of Sir Charles Clore (a dedicated friend and benefactor of the Tate Gallery who unfortunately died before discussions for a new gallery started) proposed that the works be housed together again, and Stirling and Wilford were appointed as architects in 1979 having recently completed the Staatsgallerie in Stuttgart. The decision was a triumph, not only as an example of outstanding private patronage to the arts (£1 million was also donated by the government) but also as a chance for James Stirling, one of Britain's most respected architects, to create a prominent public building in the capital city.

The brief was to hang 100 of the best paintings permanently, with additional reserve galleries, a print room for works on paper, a conservation studio and auditorium. The site determined the L-shaped extension, built between Sidney Smith's classical Tate and a red-brick military hospital. The front façade echoes neighbouring materials – red brick set within a honey-coloured stone grid. The intention was to make the Clore 'a garden building … a bit like an orangery', hence its low roofline and attention to landscaping in the foreground. The back of the building is simply yellow brick and obviously designed not to be seen. The façade is strikingly windowless, only two green windows and the entrance penetrate the grid and suggest that something occurs inside.

The entrance hall (in 'Peach' and 'Fragrance' hues) applauds Mannerism in the same way that the National Gallery extension does. The architect uses the staircase to articulate a tight space, making reference to the Scala Regia in the Vatican in Rome. On entering you walk

**Stirling Wilford Associates 1980–1985**

**Stirling Wilford Associates 1980–1985**

to your left across the hall, then right up the stairs, following the pink bannister rail, and then left, back along a landing, oriented once again by the crudely colour-coded arched window next to the entrance to the galleries. According to Chinese cosmology, demons move only in straight lines, so zig-zagging pathways are always laid in front gardens.

The galleries themselves are rather conventional in style and proportion but the beige colour of the permanent hanging walls received tremendous criticism when first revealed. The deep red (the same shade that Turner chose to hang his work against) was deemed more appropriate for the reserve galleries. Natural lighting is a success. Many of the paintings inside were painted close to the Thames, and it seemed essential to allow this true light to illuminate them. Light scoops in the ceiling bounce light on to the walls, making the middle of the gallery slightly darker than the perimeter. The overall detailing of the building is raw but that is cosmetic. When it was awarded an RIBA National Award in 1988 the jury wrote: 'the rigour with which the rather blandly detailed forms are carried through is commendable.' It is evident that the articulation of the spaces has been seriously considered, which is, after all, the architecture.

ADDRESS Millbank, London SW1 [4J 77]
CLIENT Trustees of the Tate Gallery
STRUCTURAL ENGINEER Felix J Samuely & Partners
CONTRACT VALUE £7.7 million (about the cost of one Manet painting)
SIZE 3199 square metres
TUBE Pimlico – Victoria Line
ACCESS open Monday to Saturday, 10.00–17.50; Sunday 14.00–17.50.
Closed on Bank Holidays

**Westminster**

**Stirling Wilford Associates 1980–1985**

**Westminster**

**Stirling Wilford Associates 1980–1985**

# Channel 4 Headquarters

This is a key modern building in the heart of Westminster. Sited in a stagnant corner of Victoria (boldly moving away from the Soho/West End media clique), the Channel 4 building has helped to create a new spirit in the area. The territory is stalked by the colossal 1960s' Department of the Environment blocks waiting on Death Row, the now rotting corpse of what was Westminster Hospital, the charmless DSS office just down the road and the Royal Horticultural Society buildings (1904 and 1928). Not exactly showbiz! However, this new building, comprising a major underground car park, TV studios and offices, a residential development of 100 apartments (by Lyons Sleeman + Hoare) and a garden square, should make a considerable impact on its business and residential neighbours by introducing a lively industry to the area which will generate new resources.

In plan there are four blocks around a central garden. The northern and western sides are occupied by Channel 4 and the southern and eastern sides are residential. The L-shaped office area butts up to the street but a generous recess into the corner has been given over to a dramatic entrance. The approach is across a bridge over what appears to be a glass pool, but is actually the roof of an underground studio. To your left is a stack of boxes (conference rooms) held in an elegant framework of tapered beams; to the right exterior lifts cling to a service tower and transmission antennae (the feather in the cap). The entrance itself is through a concave glass curtain – which appears to be hung from a row of curtain claws (as opposed to curtain rings) – draped between the two wings to allow a glimpse of the reception, restaurant and garden beyond.

The exterior walls of the office wings are made up largely of glass and glass blocks, clad in the lower areas with a mesh screen to reduce solar gain without creating sheer impenetrable surfaces. Elsewhere, cladding

**Richard Rogers Partnership 1991–1994**

is a dull pewter-grey aluminium and exposed steelwork is painted a rich primer red – the exact colour of the Golden Gate Bridge in San Francisco.

The contrast between all the parts of the building is what makes it so distinctive, but the elements also work together (from the outside at least) to form a varied, relatively low-level landscape rather than a solid block. The offices are identifiably different from the conference rooms, each part seeming to have a clear agenda, and the entrance holds no bars.

**Westminster**

ADDRESS Horseferry Road, London SW1 [4H 77]
STRUCTURAL ENGINEER Ove Arup & Partners
SIZE 15,000 square metres
TUBE St James' Park – Circle, District Lines
ACCESS limited

**Richard Rogers Partnership 1991–1994**

**Richard Rogers Partnership 1991–1994**

# Richmond House

A seven-storey building that conforms in every way to the surrounding architecture, from its overall height to the red-brick and stone banding on the rear façade which faces on to Norman Shaw's Old Scotland Yard building. The service stairs are housed within the stumpy yellow-brick and grey-granite columns on the Whitehall frontage. Heavy stone-mullioned bay windows reflect the austerity of the rest of Whitehall, but are no competition for Lutyens' Cenotaph which sits in the road directly in front. The best aspect is the way the building sits back from the main road, so the view down this dramatically wide road (an unusual feature in London) remains unhampered.

Charles Jencks described the scheme as 'Gothick Perpendicular meets Brutalism', a fair assessment of the government in power at the time of its construction.

ADDRESS 79 Whitehall, London W1 [1J 77]
CLIENT Department of Health and Social Security
CONTRACT VALUE £38.6 million
SIZE 15,000 square metres
TUBE Westminster – Circle, District Lines
ACCESS none

**Westminster**

**William Whitfield 1988**

**William Whitfield 1988**

# Buckingham Palace Ticket Office

Buckingham Palace has started to open its doors to visitors during August and September each year. The brief for a ticket office called for a demountable, storable structure which could be used for five years. The prefabricated timber office cabin is brought to the site in two parts (mounted on wheels) and bolted together. Birch-faced plywood ribs are bolted to the steel chassis to make the frame and then the whole is clad externally with Western red-cedar strips and sealed with yacht varnish. It is surrounded by a timber deck which floats on adjustable feet to conceal the wheels of the cabin once it is in position.

A tensile-fabric canopy covers the area defined by the edges of the deck. It is supported on two elliptical glulam timber masts (one at either end of the cabin) with a main keel beam running between them. The beam is bolted to the cabin with steel plates which slice into the laminated-timber edge above the teller windows. A series of struts attached to the main beam extends outwards horizontally, tied by vertical tensile cables to concrete blocks in the ground.

This is a building which fits the season and its setting. It uses a vocabulary of details derived from marquees, boats and elegant travelling cases – the cabin alone is like the portmanteau I imagine Her Majesty might take on holiday.

ADDRESS Lower Grosvenor Place, London SW1 [3F 77]
STRUCTURAL ENGINEER Ove Arup & Partners
TUBE Green Park – Piccadilly, Victoria Lines, then walk across the park to the Canada Gate entrance
ACCESS open in August and September only

**Westminster**

**Michael Hopkins & Partners 1994**

**Michael Hopkins & Partners 1994**

# Embankment Place, Charing Cross

The primary development in this strategic piece of city planning is 32,000 square metres of office space using the air rights above Charing Cross Station. Seven to nine storeys are suspended above the tracks, insulated from the clattering railway.

The masterplan includes 'traffic management' (Cardboard City clearance) in Embankment Place, extension of Hungerford Bridge to Charing Cross Station (an intimidating blind passageway which opens out with views on to Villiers Street), relocation of the Players' Theatre, adjustments to Embankment Gardens and to the station forecourt, and revitalisation of a pedestrianised Villiers Street. Craven Passage, beneath the station, has also been hosed down and transformed into a shopping arcade.

Design details are consistent, continuing the pretence that brick cladding reflects the street scale and granite cladding reflects the scale of other riverside buildings. Cartoon-like classical references can be found in many of the decorative motifs (bulging Doric columns on the platforms and pale green metalwork mimicking copper roofs). The giant glazed railway-shed arches crouch between service towers positioned at the four corners. The top of each tower provides stunning views across London – unfortunately reserved exclusively for the occupants of executive suites.

ADDRESS Villiers Street, London WC2 [1J 77]
STRUCTURAL ENGINEER Ove Arup & Partners
TUBE Charing Cross – Bakerloo, Jubilee, Northern Lines; Embankment – Circle, District Lines
ACCESS open

**Terry Farrell & Company 1987–1990**

**Westminster**

**Terry Farrell & Company 1987–1990**

# Sainsbury Wing
## National Gallery

The site was acquired by HM Government in 1959. Lack of funds prevented development until 1980 when the then Secretary of State, Michael Heseltine, proposed a competition to develop the site commercially with galleries on the upper floors. Ahrends Burton & Koralek were chosen to produce designs. In 1984 the Prince of Wales famously denounced ABK's scheme as 'a monstrous carbuncle on the face of a much-loved and elegant friend': not surprisingly, planning permission was refused. The present scheme was conceived early in 1985. The Sainsbury brothers offered to fund the extension and in January 1986 Venturi, Scott Brown's designs were selected. The Prince laid the foundation stone.

The aesthetics of the building (a steel and concrete frame clad in the same Portland stone as the original building designed by William Wilkins in 1838) derive from Venturi's post-modern theories, reinterpreting the past and placing it in the present. All of Wilkins' classical elements have been reproduced and then dissected. Inside, the grand stairway in charcoal-black granite has a stately presence while the vast, arched steel trusses above, mimicking the parts of a coarse Victorian train shed, are just some of the many incongruities that lurk in the building.

Venturi's own words sum up the building and his attitude towards his architecture: 'It is very sophisticated. You have to be "cultured" to like it.' How many of those whom he refers to as 'the relatively unsophisticated people' who visit the gallery are prepared to swallow that?

ADDRESS Trafalgar Square, London SW1 [1H 77]
ASSOCIATED UK ARCHITECT Sheppard Robson Architects
TUBE Charing Cross – Bakerloo, Jubilee, Northern Lines
ACCESS open Monday to Saturday, 10.00–18.00; Sunday 14.00–18.00. Closed on Bank Holidays

Westminster

**Venturi, Scott Brown & Associates, Inc. 1988–1991**

**Venturi, Scott Brown & Associates, Inc. 1988–1991**

# Sackler Galleries
**Royal Academy of Arts**

Sir Norman Foster adds his name to a short but distinguished list of architects who have contributed to the evolution of the Royal Academy. Burlington House was built in 1666. The front elevation was remodelled by Colen Campbell from 1717–1720, with a garden façade by Samuel Ware added in 1815 and a gallery extension by Sidney Smirke in 1867. A gap, almost 5 metres wide, between the garden façade and Smirke's extension is the site for Foster's contribution, which provides new circulation up to the previously isolated Diploma Galleries on the third storey.

From the atmosphere of a narrow Victorian alley-way at ground level, visitors are rapidly transported by a glass-walled, hydraulic lift up to a new public space. The journey up through three floors past the newly renovated exteriors of Smirke and Ware is breathtaking (it could quite easily be 30 floors). At the top you are dazzled by bright white light through translucent glass all around, and the vast, sculpted head of a Greek god resting on the parapet of Smirke's façade creates a bizarre and dramatic sense of scale and great distance.

Stepping out of the lift into the public gallery and meeting place, you are free to wander and look at Gibson's sculptures which sit along the same parapet. At the end, across a delicate glass bridge, is a cool, open ante-room where you can sit and view the Royal Academy's most valuable possession, Michelangelo's *Virgin and Child with Infant St John*, and catch another look back along the sculpture gallery. This series of spaces, which floats structurally independent between the old buildings, is simply defined by light and subtle changes in materials. Glazed edges around the floor surfaces help to make the distinction between the old and new building techniques.

The three Diploma Galleries (now the Sackler Galleries) were gutted, their flat roofs demolished and two barrel-vaulted ceilings with roof lights

**Westminster**

**Foster Associates 1989–1991**

**Foster Associates 1989–1991**

installed. As a conservation measure, air quality is carefully controlled: air is distributed very slowly across the art works and wall surfaces. Roof lights provide UV filtration and natural light is controlled by fritted glass and a series of louvres that opens and closes depending on the intensity of the light. This solution has proved unsatisfactory and is currently being reassessed.

Visitors can leave the galleries by descending the staircase. It has the elegant sweep of a grand stairway but, like a fire escape, it provides a winding route down through the gap with views through the windows of the old garden façade into the offices of the gallery. There is a sense of being underground when you look up and see shadows of footsteps through the sand-blasted glass stair treads over your head.

Extensive use of different types of glass (a Foster trademark) has allowed as much natural light as possible to filter down through the gap while the vertical movement through it allows us to see the old façades in a new and more detailed way, giving a whole new meaning to scale and proportion, comfort without upholstery, conservation without conservatism.

ADDRESS Piccadilly, London W1 [1F 77]
CLIENT Royal Academy of Arts
STRUCTURAL ENGINEER YRM Anthony Hunt Associates
HISTORIC BUILDINGS CONSULTANT Julian Harrap Associates
CONTRACT VALUE £5.2 million
TUBE Piccadilly Circus – Bakerloo, Piccadilly Lines; Green Park – Piccadilly, Victoria Lines
ACCESS open 10.00–17.30 daily

**Foster Associates 1989–1991**

# Jigsaw, New Bond Street

Jigsaw's philosophy since it began manufacturing and retailing women's clothes in Hampstead, Putney and Richmond 23 years ago has been, 'to sell affordable, fashionable clothes in stylish surroundings … which help to create a calm shopper who is unafraid of buying.' The clothes are simple and feminine, designed to form the core of one's wardrobe rather than to make any wild statements – New Bond Street is home to designers such as Hermes, Chanel and Versace and more recently DKNY and Prada – so this most recent outlet puts the high street store into the flagship league.

At its Knightsbridge store Branson Coates tried to liven up the Jigsaw image by playing on the decadent and frivolous aspects of shopping. Here the architecture responds more closely to the company ethos and to the current tempo of other New Bond Street residents by providing a calm backdrop. Natural light floods through the double-height glass frontage to illuminate simple, sand-blasted acrylic screens that serve to separate types and colours of garment and define a clear means of circulation through the length of the deep site. The materials are, in the architect's own word, 'sensual'.

When taking on the conversion of an old electronics store made up of two adjoining houses in one of London's most prestigious shopping streets, John Pawson had to retrieve what he could from the site, retaining existing structural columns and walls and 'taking things out, not putting them in'. The imposition of order and calm is central to his design philosophy. Here such surfaces as the Portland stone on the ground floor have been laid in a continuous seamless plane rather than in tile form while the timber planks in the basement were chosen to be as wide and as long as possible, reminding us that timber comes from trees not from Homebase. The staircase has been enhanced to achieve maximum impact with

**John Pawson 1996**

**John Pawson 1996**

a minimum of special effects. The solid stone steps take on a surreal weightlessness, appearing to be detached from the perimeter wall and lit from beneath along this edge. A few pieces of specially designed furniture are placed as props for accessories, to provide a surface on which really unafraid shoppers can compose an outfit, or for weary companions to sit on.

This kind of project, like most work in the retail and restaurant sectors, provides the architect with an opportunity to indulge in materials and try out devices in a controlled environment. As the client's description indicates, the objectives of retail are clear and calculated. The architect's brief (and Pawson answers it sumptuously) is quite simply to seduce.

ADDRESS 126–127 New Bond Street, London W1 [6F 61]
CLIENT Jigsaw (Robinson Webster Holdings Limited)
STRUCTURAL ENGINEER S B Tietz & Partners
CONTRACT VALUE £1 million
SIZE 660 square metres
TUBE Bond Street – Central, Jubilee Lines
ACCESS during shop-opening hours

Westminster

**John Pawson 1996**

**John Pawson 1996**

# South London

**Peckham Square**

A project funded by the government's Urban Partnership Fund, this is part of a regeneration strategy to give a visible injection of energy on to blighted inner-city areas. The scheme proposes a suitably flamboyant solution in the form of a market place, street theatre and general meeting place, beneath one roof. The 35-metre span of the canopy covers a raised and paved area (pattern designed by Alison Turnbull) sandwiched between boarded-up shop fronts from which its steel supporting members grow. Tension rods provide stability across the span. The roof area is covered in plywood and sealed with a waterproof membrane. Meanwhile, two circles are punched out to admit shafts of light and … torrents of rain, drenching the homeless people who have made it their roof and their space.

It is becoming increasingly evident that architecture is capable of taking on a dynamic role within the life of a city. A roof, in this instance, does not in fact fulfil its role as shelter, though it does act as a signpost (to what is ambiguous). It also acts as a scientific instrument. The architects worked with lighting designer Ron Haseldon to develop a 'meteorologically active' system – in other words, a barometer. Gels giving 16 colour variants illuminate the underside of the arch and change according to atmospheric conditions.

ADDRESS Peckham High Street, London SE15 [1G 95]
CLIENT London Borough of Southwark
STRUCTURAL ENGINEER Ove Arup & Partners
BR Peckham Rye from London Bridge
ACCESS open

**Troughton McAslan 1994**

**Troughton McAslan 1994**

# Vauxhall Cross

Vauxhall Cross is MI6's headquarters. Until they moved here, the secret services had been housed inconspicuously in undistinguishable 1960s office buildings around London. A new image is being nurtured.

This is a bespoke (as opposed to a speculative) office building. The brief included the construction of a landscaped river wall and a public riverside walkway. Three main blocks, containing nine floors, step back from low-rise bunkers at garden level, rising in cold symmetry to a bow window, reminiscent of the river frontage at Charing Cross (see page 86), but this time crowned with menacing concrete spikes. There is an equal proportion of dark-green-glazed curtain walling and precast pigmented concrete panels (each weighing 5–8 tonnes). It is the largest precast-concrete cladding contract to date in the UK.

The building is utterly impermeable – the façade allows no insight into the human activities inside. These appearances are by no means deceptive: built into the concrete framework is a 'Faraday Cage' – a mesh which prevents electromagnetic information from passing in or out of the building. An anonymous site has gained a theatrically-ominous building – apt that its neighbour to the west should be the Nine Elms Cold Store.

ADDRESS Albert Embankment, London SE1 [5J 77]
CLIENT Regalian Properties
STRUCTURAL ENGINEER Ove Arup & Partners
CONTRACT VALUE £125 million
SIZE 12,000 square metres (site area)
TUBE Vauxhall – Victoria Line
BR Vauxhall from Waterloo
ACCESS none

**South London**

**Terry Farrell & Company 1990–1993**

**Terry Farrell & Company 1990–1993**

# Waterloo International Terminal

'The Gateway to Europe' is one of the longest railway stations in the world, with the capacity to handle up to 15 million passengers a year. The architects' ambition was to capture the spirit of such heroic engineers as Isambard Kingdom Brunel – who created large-span glass- and iron-roofed railway stations more than a century ago – and to celebrate the Channel Tunnel rail link to the rest of Europe.

Five new tracks were set out by British Rail; these determined the geometry and shape of the whole scheme. The new building is made up of four components. At the bottom, a reinforced-concrete box accommodates the car park which spans the Underground lines and forms the foundation for the terminal. On top of this concrete box sits a two-storey viaduct supporting the 400-metre-long platforms. This part must bear the weight of the 800-tonne trains and their braking force. Third, brick vaults beneath the existing station were repaired to accommodate back-up services. The fourth and most prominent component is the roof, though it absorbed only 10 per cent of the overall budget. It extends the full length of the 400-metre trains, providing shelter for all the passengers like a vast scaly sleeve. Unfortunately, it does not crash into the existing patchwork of railway sheds but stops at an awkward distance from the main Waterloo entrance. However, it happily disregards the apartment and office blocks along its length, clipping the corners of any buildings that stand in its way.

The complex structure is essentially a flattened three-pin bowstring arch, distorted to follow the curve and changing width of the platforms. A series of diminishing compressive tubes is employed to cope with any movement. Pressed, profiled, stainless-steel tapered tubes define the bays and give expression to the lightweight structure. In order to avoid cutting 2520 panels of glass to size, at vast expense, a 'loose-fit' glazing system

**Nicholas Grimshaw & Partners 1991–1993**

**South London**

Nicholas Grimshaw & Partners 1991–1993

of overlapping standard-size glass sheets had to be devised with a concertina joint to deal with the twist in the structure.

The whole roof system was thoroughly tested before going on site – a 1:1 model was weather tested with the help of high-pressure hoses and an aircraft engine to simulate rain and wind, followed by a 16-week construction dress rehearsal to ensure that everything would run according to plan on site.

**South London**

ADDRESS Waterloo Station, London SE1 [2K 77]
CLIENT British Rail
ROOF ENGINEER YRM Anthony Hunt Associates
TRAFFIC AND PASSENGER FLOW Sir Alexander Gibb & Partners
CONTRACT VALUE £120 million
TUBE Waterloo – Bakerloo, Northern Lines
ACCESS open; the interior is open only to travellers to Europe

**Nicholas Grimshaw & Partners 1991–1993**

# Pavilion
## Hayward Gallery

A clause in the gallery's insurance prohibited the consumption of alcohol in places where loaned works of art were on display. This left no space in which to hold functions for sponsors. The solution is this timber structure (inspired by the traditional barns of the Pennsylvanian Amish sect) which sits like a huge freight container on one of the sculpture balconies overlooking Waterloo Bridge.

Originally designed as a temporary structure and built in 28 days, the entire shed is clad in sterling board and stained a rich, burnt red. On a good day when the 4-metre full-height doors on the north elevation are flung open, the interior brims with natural light; artificial lighting is by the high-street catalogue store Argos. Interior columns are wrapped in rope to avoid splinters at hand and shoulder level.

The architects have got the most out of the one material by paying attention to finish and detailing, and the pavilion is as self-assured as any so-called permanent structure, particularly the one on which it rests. The pavilion has now been appropriated as a permanent feature of the Hayward Gallery; it currently houses a café.

The same architects have refurbished The People's Palace restaurant in the neighbouring Royal Festival Hall.

ADDRESS South Bank, London SE1 [K1 77]
STRUCTURAL ENGINEER Whitby & Bird
CONTRACT VALUE £52,000
TUBE Waterloo – Bakerloo, Northern Lines (signs to Hayward Gallery)
ACCESS gallery open 10.00–18.00 Thursday to Monday; 10.00–20.00 Tuesday and Wednesday

South London

**Allies & Morrison 1994**

**South London**

**Allies & Morrison 1994**

# Broadwall, Coin Street Housing

A site with a unique social and political history, it was acquired in 1984 for £1 million from the Greater London Council by a group of Waterloo and Southwark residents calling themselves the Coin Street Community Builders. A separate housing association, the Coin Street Secondary Housing Co-operative, was subsequently set up to get funding to develop individual housing sites. Once a scheme has been completed, it is run by its own co-operative, drawing tenants of mixed incomes and origins from Lambeth and Southwark. All adults are made members of the co-operative, responsible for setting and paying rents to the Secondary Housing Co-operative. Each tenant is sent on a 12-week training programme to develop the necessary managerial skills before moving in.

Because of the poor quality of the detailing in the initial schemes, subsequent housing has been commissioned on the basis of architectural competitions. Broadwall is the result of this policy.

The brief called for 25 dwellings comprising ten family houses with gardens, five two-bedroom three-person flats and ten one-bedroom two-person flats. The layout of the scheme demonstrates a logical and effectively urban way to accommodate a mixture of people with different housing needs, addressing an ingrained scepticism towards building types such as the tower block.

The smaller flats for two people have been grouped together in a nine-storey tower at the north end of the site (the head); the flats may lack gardens but they do have a stunning view across the river. An elevator serves each floor individually for privacy and security. The neck and tail at the south end of the scheme is formed by two four-storey blocks for the larger flats; the main body is a row of 11 three-storey family houses with direct access to a new park on the west side of the scheme. All the flats and houses have spacious kitchens and living rooms with a western

**Lifschutz Davidson Design 1995**

**Lifschutz Davidson Design 1995**

outlook through full-height windows, and balconies with enough room to sit out on. Bedrooms are located against the impenetrable brick wall on the street side.

A generous budget (80 per cent of which came from a Housing Corporation grant) allowed unusual attention to be paid to the quality of detailing, which uses a wide (some might say extravagant) selection of materials. This should increase the project's longevity although the scheme is too expensive to serve as a model for other housing-association developments.

The site sits at the heart of a goldmine of approved architectural proposals: the Bankside Tate Gallery of Modern Art by Herzog & de Meuron (see page 340), the reconstructed Globe Theatre (see page 122) and the OXO Tower building with its workshops, shops and high-profile top-floor restaurant for Harvey Nichols (also designed by Lifschutz Davidson). It benefits from the new pedestrian and road route linking Blackfriars Bridge with the South Bank complex – a series of anonymous back streets has been transformed into a clearly defined avenue by new lighting, paving, bollards and flags designed by various artists. The opening of a Jubilee Line station at Southwark (see page 330) will also undoubtedly enhance services to the area.

ADDRESS off Stamford Street, London SE1 [1A 78]
CLIENT Coin Street Secondary Housing Co-operative
STRUCTURAL ENGINEER Buro Happold Consulting Engineers
SIZE 27 units on a 0.15-hectare site (the whole site is 5.3 hectares)
TUBE Waterloo – Bakerloo, Northern Lines
ACCESS none to individual homes; see the project from Stamford Street

**Lifschutz Davidson Design 1995**

**Lifschutz Davidson Design 1995**

**Bankside Lofts**

Having worked together on apartments located above Sir Terence Conran's Mezzo restaurant development in Soho, czwg and the Manhattan Loft Corporation continue their architect-developer relationship here at Bankside to create a luxury housing block in an area set to become a new economic and cultural pressure point in central London. The developer-as-speculator cannot fail to strike gold here with the new Tate Gallery of Modern Art just across the road due for completion in 2000 (see page 340), the Globe Theatre just a short stroll along the riverfront (see page 122), the proximity of the Young and Old Vic theatres in Waterloo, and a new Jubilee Line station at Southwark to be open by spring 1999 (see page 330), let alone all the retail/restaurant paraphernalia these developments will spawn.

Bankside Lofts brings up-to-date czwg's portfolio of distinctive luxury housing developments located in raw urban landscapes to help trigger these areas into becoming attractive new commercial and residential districts (see Cascades in Docklands and the Circle at Butler's Wharf, page 304 and page 144 respectively).

But here, the post-modern extremes with which Piers Gough (the G in czwg) so mischievously flirted in the 1980s have been distilled into a late-1990s post-post-modern mould where classical-architecture references give way to a more restrained, organic approach. The phased development comprises a combination of converted and new buildings set around a new raised garden screened from the road by a breaker of timber baulks. A red-brick Italianate ex-cocoa mill is at the centre of the group (phase 1). The snail-plan spiral tower is an extension upwards and sideways of an existing 1950s building (phases 2 and 3). Its generally north-facing orientation enables apartments on the upper floors to have views of the river, with a stepped effect falling away to the south reducing the bulk

**CZWG Architects 1998**

**CZWG Architects 1998**

of the tower on the skyline. The stepping also exaggerates a hierarchy, with the penthouse apartment unquestionably forming a summit. The curve in the plan means that retail spaces at ground level benefit from panoramic fish-eye frontages. While having a touch of the Trump Tower about it, the tower's yellow-rendered frame and the immense metal-framed windows of the double-height loft spaces create a more industrial edge. On the south side of the tower are a newly restored seventeenth-century cottage (once the home of Nell Gwynne) and a new brick office building. On the east and south sides of the garden is another newly built loft building (distinguished by its grey-rendered elevations) angled to gain views north across the river (phases 4 and 5).

Gough's sense of abandon is evident in his cartoon-like use of colour and scale and the theatricality of the form. He has risen to the occasion on behalf of Manhattan Lofts by designing a mini-skyscraper for a Dick Tracey set rather than just a block of flats for Southwark; the advertising hoarding on top adds the final graphic touch.

ADDRESS corner of Hopton Street and Holland Street, London SE1 [1B 78]
CLIENT Manhattan Loft Corporation
STRUCTURAL ENGINEERS Vincent Grant (phases 1–3); Dewhurst Macfarlane & Partners (phases 4 and 5)
TUBE Southwark – Jubilee Line Extension from spring 1999
ACCESS ground floor only

**CZWG Architects 1998**

**CZWG Architects 1998**

# The Jerwood Space

A Victorian red-brick school building has been restructured to provide a permanent gallery space, four dance and theatre rehearsal studios and five lettable studio spaces for artists and designers. Office facilities are attached to each rehearsal space so a small company can set up camp for the duration of its rehearsal time. The ground-floor spaces can be linked together and to the courtyard at the side through tall, partially glazed partition doors.

The client was keen to preserve as much of the original building as possible, while the limited budget meant that any new proposals had to focus on essential needs. So Paxton Locher's scheme is composed of broad brush strokes which make maximum use of space and natural light, and clarify use. The new main entrance and gallery occupy former bike sheds in the space linking the old flanking entrances on Union Street (the 'boys' and 'girls' keystones have been incorporated into outdoor benches). This long block makes use of original steel roof trusses and north-facing roof lights with the addition of an entirely glazed back wall facing on to an internal sculpture court. The client was concerned that the glazing would reduce the amount of hanging space within the gallery, so removable display panels have been designed to attach to the glazing panels when required. A café at the west end of the block also opens on to the planted courtyard.

Paxton Locher excel at exploiting deep awkward spaces without making them feel cramped or claustrophobic (see page 214). Their strategy is to capture natural light sources wherever possible and create clear sightlines between spaces, using glass for walls rather than solid partitions. The method comes into play in the main office area, located at a difficult junction between the front gallery block and the rehearsal studios in the main body of the school. At some point a mezzanine level

**Paxton Locher Architects 1998**

South London

**Paxton Locher Architects 1998**

had been inserted into this area forming small box-like rooms. Now, with fully glazed partitions and the use of an existing exterior double-height window, the ground- floor reception and director's office on the mezzanine level both benefit from an unobstructed vista through to the gallery, courtyard and entrance.

The main body of the old building remains reassuringly raw, its robust features – high ceilings, tall windows, glazed-tile walls and scrubbed concrete corridor floors – preserved. An application for lottery funding at an advanced stage called for the provision of a lift for disabled access. Responding to the client's request for something 'butch', the architects have encased the east elevation in glass with gangways at first- and second-floor levels linking directly to a new brick and glass lift tower.

Reconditioning old buildings for new uses became something of a joke in the 1980s; a retained structure would be disembowelled to make way for new slab floors and suspended ceilings slung crudely across exisiting window openings. This project shows that a more intelligent approach may be taken and that some old buildings can benefit from a new lease of life.

ADDRESS 171 Union Street, London SE1 [1B 78]
CLIENT The Jerwood Foundation (with financial assistance from the Arts Council Lottery Fund)
STRUCTURAL ENGINEER Elliott Wood Partnership
CONTRACT VALUE £0.5 million
SIZE 2300 square metres
TUBE Southwark – Jubilee Line Extension from spring 1999
ACCESS gallery open 10.00–18.00 daily

**Paxton Locher Architects 1998**

**South London**

**Paxton Locher Architects 1998**

**Globe Theatre**

This is the oldest new building in London (even older than the British Library) and the first thatched building to be constructed in central London since the Great Fire of 1666. Its history dates back to 1598-99, when the original round wooden theatre was built by Cuthbert and Richard Burbage with master craftsman Peter Streete. The Globe was named after its sign, which showed Hercules carrying the world on his shoulders, not, as is often thought, because of its polygonal plan (suggesting a sphere) with the central pit around the stage open to the heavens. The theatre was destroyed in 1613 – it is thought by a cannon fired during a performance of shareholder William Shakespeare's *Henry VIII*, which set the thatch alight. It was rebuilt immediately on the original foundations but was closed by the Puritans in 1642 and demolished two years later.

The idea of rebuilding the theatre was resuscitated by actor Sam Wanamaker, who established the Globe Playhouse Trust in 1970. In the same year Southwark Council offered the trust this 1.2-hectare site, only 180 metres from the original. Seventeen years later the site was cleared and a diaphragm wall constructed to protect it from the River Thames so construction could begin.

Peter McCurdy's team worked for six years on the research, detailed design and fabrication of the timber structure using panoramic maps, illustrations of theatres of the period, and contracts, accounts and surveys of buildings of a similar date. From this analysis the diameter was established. Twenty bays form a galleried perimeter wall, each three storeys high and thatched in Norfolk reed with lime plaster. The stage in the centre is covered by a canopy spanning 14 metres supported on two 8.5-metre-high timber columns (made from trees found in the Scottish Borders and in Norfolk). Having completed 15 bays, work began on the

**Theo Crosby at Pentagram 1997**

**Theo Crosby at Pentagram 1997**

stage and Tyring House (the backstage area). At this point the stage roof was redesigned in line with further research that suggested a larger, projecting pentice roof and a more complex 'heavens' structure (the highly decorated ceiling above the stage).

Remaining true to sixteenth-century materials, the craftsmen used unseasoned green oak. The young timber is liable to move considerably as it ages, so each scribed joint is unique and identified with the carpenter's numeral, as would have been the case in 1598.

Can the process of faithful reconstruction inspire the way we approach contemporary buildings, or is it motivated by the 'Disney factor'? Unfortunately both the founder of the project, Sam Wanamaker, and the chief architect, Theo Crosby, died during the building process. However, master craftsman Peter McCurdy maintains that the building provides a unique forum for academic and archaeological research and investigation into the design and construction of timber frames as well as a platform for actors and audiences alike to explore a more authentic staging of Shakespeare's theatre.

ADDRESS Park Street, Bankside, London SE1 [1C 78]
CLIENT The Globe Playhouse Trust
SPECIALIST CRAFTSMEN McCurdy & Co
STRUCTURAL ENGINEER Buro Happold Consulting Engineers
CONTRACT VALUE £30 million
SIZE 30.5 metres diameter, 91.5 metres circumference
TUBE London Bridge – Northern Line; Southwark – Jubilee Line
Extension from spring 1999
ACCESS open for performances

**South London**

**Theo Crosby at Pentagram 1997**

# Butlers Wharf infrastructure

Conran Roche has been leading a comprehensive revitalisation strategy to rebuild the infrastructure of Butlers Wharf and restore many of its 17 Grade II-listed buildings. The site, acquired in 1984 for a mere £5 million, is within the London Bridge Conservation Area. The overall plan is to build up a community where people will want to live and work again, with leisure, retail, office, residential and industrial facilities.

At the beginning of this century the area was occupied by flour, corn and rice merchants. Everything and everybody was covered in a heavy dusting of white powder. Many of the warehouses were then used to store spices, and a few of these are still in operation and have continued life as normal as building works have been carried out around them – you can still smell the pungent aroma of cinnamon and nutmeg as you walk down Gainsford Street. There is a peculiarly ghostly air since much of the area lies derelict, evoking the atmosphere of Charles Dickens' *Oliver Twist*. The area is still infinitely enticing because there are still bits to explore.

The new infrastructure includes the pedestrianisation of Shad Thames and Lafone Street, the refurbishment of existing streets to increase pavement widths, and the upgrading of street services, such as lighting. The quayside and river edge have been completely rejuvenated with a promenade of York stone and a pontoon to give access to the rather-too-infrequent riverbus service.

It does seem that a rigorous plan has been set out to integrate new activities into the rich but decaying building fabric. Diverse sectors of society have settled in – students from the London School of Economics (see page 134) live next to the inhabitants of luxury apartments, which sit next to deserted Victorian warehouses, a community nursery, workshops and the Design Museum (see page 130). This will increasingly become an area

**Conran Roche 1988–1990**

where people will want to hang out, particularly if more efficient transport links are implemented.

The Butlers Wharf Building is at the heart of the development. Other buildings in the development (all the work of Conran Roche) include Nutmeg House (Gainsford Street; the architects' offices upstairs, a community nursery and shop on the ground floor), the Cardamon Building (Shad Thames; five Grade II-listed warehouses rehabilitated as 64 residential units connected by bridges to the back of the Butlers Wharf Building), the Coriander Building (Gainsford Street; two Victorian warehouses converted to office space, now linked by a glazed service core), and Cinnamon Wharf (Shad Thames; a seven-storey warehouse converted into 66 flats).

ADDRESS Butlers Wharf, London SE1 [2F 79]
CLIENT Butlers Wharf Limited
CONTRACT VALUE £6.5 million
SIZE 4.5-hectare site
TUBE Tower Hill – Circle, District Lines, walk over Tower Bridge
ACCESS open

**Conran Roche 1988–1990**

**South London**

**Conran Roche 1988–1990**

# Design Museum

The Design Museum was set up by Terence Conran (founder of Habitat Stores and the Conran Shop) and Stephen Bayley to explain the function, appearance and marketing of consumer goods. The intention is to help to raise the awareness of design standards in everything from kettles to cars, from the earliest days of mass production. It also provides a resource to inform the work of the present-day design industry. It can be seen as a monument to the changing status of design during the Thatcher era. The objects in the museum are design classics which have now become cult objects – strangely contradictory.

The disused 1950s warehouse overlooking the Thames has been reconstructed to accommodate a permanent Study Collection with limited reference material available at interactive computer terminals, a space for temporary exhibitions, a library, a lecture theatre and the Blueprint Café. The project started as a refurbishment but it proved cheaper to demolish and rebuild much of the original building because of a new VAT ruling on all construction except new building in the 1984 government budget.

The Study Collection is housed on the top floor in a double-height space saturated in natural light, which causes the neutral English-oak and marble floors and white walls to glow. The temporary gallery is the usual white space that can be changed to exhibit anything from the corporate logos of Raymond Loewy to the furniture of Eileen Gray. Both the interior spaces were designed by Stanton Williams.

The Blueprint Café, designed by Terence Conran, is the only facility that really makes use of the original building and its prime location, by employing the layered frontage. The entrance, up a wide white stairwell, rather like the echoing approach to a swimming baths, leads customers into the open café area with its glass frontage and a terrace overlooking the Thames. The proximity of the water and the coolness of the space

**Conran Roche 1987–1989**

**Conran Roche 1987–1989**

make you feel like you could be dining luxuriously on a cruise liner rather than on dry land.

The museum itself, once a red-brick building, now rendered and painted white, undoubtedly pays tribute to the simplicity of the modern movement. The café, on the other hand, is a product of Conran's noble quest since the early 1980s to educate our ignorant British palates with Mediterranean cooking. However, given the situation, I think it would be more of an education to eat something that Mies van der Rohe or Mr Olivetti might have had for lunch.

**South London**

ADDRESS Shad Thames, London SE1 [2F 79]
CLIENT The Conran Foundation
CONTRACT VALUE £5.1 million
SIZE 3700 square metres gross
TUBE Tower Hill – Circle, District Lines, walk over Tower Bridge
ACCESS open 10.30–17.30 daily

**Conran Roche 1987–1989**

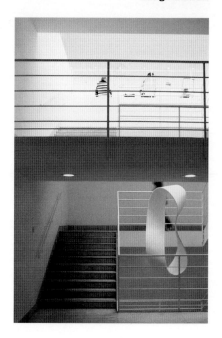

**Conran Roche 1987–1989**

# Student Residence
**London School of Economics**

This is a six-storey building with 280 student rooms served by four separate cores – each stairwell gives access to a pair of flats at each level. Each flat comprises six single study-bedrooms with built-in furniture and storage facilities – though they are rather cramped, it was essential to make maximum use of the limited space – and a communal dining/living area with a balcony facing south on to Gainsford Street. The new block could be mistaken for more luxurious apartments but the orange plastic chairs and piles of laundry that spew out on to the balconies give it that authentic hall-of-residence feel.

It is to be hoped that other members of the community will respond to the student presence here and create affordable services for them, thereby enriching the diversity of the area. There is certainly no shortage of available space.

South London

ADDRESS Gainsford Street, London SE1 [2F 79]
CLIENT London School of Economics
CONTRACT VALUE £5.3 million
SIZE 280 student rooms
TUBE Tower Hill – Circle, District Lines, walk over Tower Bridge
ACCESS none

**Conran Roche 1987–1989**

**Conran Roche 1987–1989**

**Camera Press**

A very tight budget (£30 per square foot as opposed to a more usual £60) and a fast building schedule determined the design approach to what was once a 1960s warehouse. It has been gracefully transformed into a photographic gallery on the ground floor with laboratories at the back, an open-plan office and meeting room on the first floor and a photographic library on the top mezzanine floor.

The two main features of the original structure – the concrete frame and the huge, timber loading-bay doors – have been maintained but adapted to give the building a new character. The most immediate requirement for the client was the creation of a warm, dry envelope. The concrete frame was stripped down to its skeleton, then the side and rear elevations were infilled with Snowcem panels with stainless-steel edging bands. The Queen Elizabeth Street elevation is glazed from floor to ceiling on the ground floor and the upper two storeys are infilled with untreated Iroko timber panels and glazing. The timber is an excellent insulator. Upper-storey corner balconies hang out over the pavement, unsupported at ground-floor level, so that when viewed from Lafone Street the building appears to be collaged on to the buildings behind rather than slicing abruptly through them.

Inside, the architects have been equally creative with but not preoccupied by the limited resources. In the gallery, loading-bay doors and fair-faced-blockwork walls provide hanging space; the flooring is oak. Similarly, upstairs oak floors are the only lavish feature among an assortment of neatly detailed scaffold pipes as door handles and cheap, building-site light fittings. Another recycled door resting on shorter door sections becomes the boardroom table. The mezzanine floor is approached via an industrial spiral staircase and is accommodated within the height of the new profiled metal-decking pitched roof. All services are

**Panter Hudspith 1993**

South London

**Panter Hudspith 1993**

contained within galvanised pipes and pinned to the concrete frame.

The natural transformation of the external materials over time sets the building apart from other converted warehouses. The approach does not try to ape urban industrial styles (inert white spaces with aluminium duct trim) but rather resembles a rural barn which responds to and is affected by the elements – the timber will gradually become bleached by the sun and each of the exterior concrete panels has the quality of a blank canvas waiting to be painted by the rain.

ADDRESS 21/23 Queen Elizabeth Street, London SE1 [2F 79]
CLIENT Camera Press
STRUCTURAL ENGINEER Cameron Taylor Bedford
CONTRACT VALUE £350,000
SIZE 990 square metres
TUBE Tower Hill – Circle, District Lines, walk over Tower Bridge
ACCESS ground-floor Tom Blau Gallery open Monday to Friday 09.00–18.00

**Panter Hudspith 1993**

**Panter Hudspith 1993**

# David Mellor Building

Still known as the David Mellor Building, it is now more precisely the Sir Terence Conran HQ and home (on the penthouse floor). Sitting at the epicentre of the Conran empire which dominates the area, the building contrasts with the indigenous building stock but reflects the character of both the original client and his successor. Mellor is to kitchen utensils what Conran is to the rest of our homes. He had specific functions in mind for the spaces that were created, namely a 3-metre-high glazed shop/showroom on the ground floor, with workshops and dimly glazed offices on the middle floors and a residence for himself on the top floor, in order to enjoy privacy and the surrounding views of the dock.

Services are held in the gap between the main rectangular concrete frame of the building and Cinnamon Wharf on the north side. A solid, slate-grey stair tower is attached to the south side like the amputated limb of some much larger and more monstrous construction. The heavy, slate effect is created by lead-wrapped panels hung on to the internal metal frame. Textured circular columns penetrate the glazed space on the ground floor. The materials used are not gleaming white and stainless steel as 1980s' kitchen etiquette dictates; rather they connote an element of rural craftsmanship but on a factory scale (many of the items that were sold were made in Mellor's Derbyshire factory, also designed by Michael Hopkins). The Conran shop has had no trouble in adapting its look to the distinctive premises.

ADDRESS Shad Thames, London SE1 [2F 79]
CLIENT David Mellor
TUBE Tower Hill – Circle, District Lines, walk over Tower Bridge
ACCESS to shop

**Michael Hopkins & Partners 1990**

South London

**Michael Hopkins & Partners 1990**

**Horselydown Square**

The scheme comprises four apartment buildings incorporating shops and two office buildings. The concept was to respond to the scale of the surrounding streets and to emulate the density and life of the city by providing a mixture of uses. Two new squares and cross-routes allow public access through the block and provide a connection to the river walk. At the centre of the main square is a fountain designed by Tony Donaldson, surrounded by shops. The smaller square is cobbled, bringing together parts of the old city such as the Anchor Tap pub and one of the new office blocks. The two squares are linked by a narrow passageway. The dense labyrinthine effect of the overall plan has also penetrated the design of the flats, which spiral up to three storeys high, some with roof terraces or balconies and others culminating in turrets looking over into neighbouring streets. The exterior walls are rendered and painted terracotta and window frames are a brilliant blue.

The composition and colour are reminiscent of an Italian hill town, although this being newly developed Bermondsey, the development lacks the deep-rooted community and dusty, sun-drenched air. A similar palette is used at a private house by the same architect at 50 Southern Row, London W10.

ADDRESS Horselydown Lane, London SE1 [17 79]
CLIENT Berkley House plc
CONTRACT VALUE £17 million
SIZE 14,200 square metres total
TUBE Tower Hill – Circle, District Lines, walk over Tower Bridge
ACCESS to shops

South London

**Wickham & Associates 1989**

**South London**

**Wickham & Associates 1989**

**The Circle**

Approaching from either end of Queen Elizabeth Street, an unsuspecting visitor to the area will be unceremoniously engulfed in a vat of cobalt blue. While working out whether you are in an interior or an exterior space, tell-tale signs like the clouds above your head will indicate that this is simply a widening in the road. Appropriately industrial in scale, the glazed-brick façades of this housing scheme form a circular courtyard (hence its name). The idea was to create more pavement in an area renowned for its canyon streets – and a dropping-off point for cars, essential for the huge loads of shopping residents amass in out-of-town hypermarkets, these being their only lifeline if retail units on the ground floor remain empty. The heavy cargo is then transported via one of two lifts in either the north or south lobby up to one of the seven storeys, along a corridor and into a conventional 1930s prototype flat.

No decorative expense has been spared: diagonal glazing bars on painfully small windows and wavy brickwork parapets along the street elevations. There is no disguising the fact that this project is simply a piece of theatre. I half expected to be heckled by retired seamen from the bulky timber balconies that run diagonally up the façades, but there was no sign of such vibrant life. The Circle demonstrates that cosmetics are not enough to rethink a modern way of living.

ADDRESS Queen Elizabeth Street, London SE1 [2F 79]
CLIENT Jacob's Island plc
CONTRACT VALUE £32 million
SIZE 42,500 square metres of floor space
TUBE Tower Hill – Circle, District Lines, walk over Tower Bridge
ACCESS to shops

South London

**CZWG Architects 1987–1989**

**CZWG Architects 1987–1989**

**China Wharf**

This was CZWG's first big apartment building and has become quite a landmark on the Thames. Wedged in between two refurbished Victorian warehouses, it has three faces which reflect the types of industrial building in the area. One street façade is of London-stock brick, matching Reeds Wharf next door. The entrance courtyard façade has a scalloped face faintly echoing the scale and appearance of the industrial silos that once stood nearby. Windows are twisted towards the sun and away from neighbours. The scooped bottoms of each scallop, painted bright red, have provided superior lavatory facilities for the local birdlife.

The river façade is more pagoda (owing something to its name) than Victorian London, its bold red arches emphasising the window type and then peeling off to provide visual support for balconies. The interior is arranged on a scissor plan so each flat has a view of the river and a private space at the back. The interior detailing is 1980s kitsch, the exterior a post-modern cartoon.

CZWG's most recently completed housing scheme can be seen at Dundee Wharf, located above the Limehouse Tunnel and off Limehouse Causeway and Narrow Street.

ADDRESS Mill Street, London SE1 [2F 79]
CLIENT Jacob's Island plc, Harry Neal Limited
STRUCTURAL ENGINEER Alan Baxter Associates
CONTRACT VALUE £2.5 million
SIZE 1800 square metres
TUBE Tower Hill – Circle, District Lines, walk over Tower Bridge
ACCESS none

South London

**CZWG Architects 1988**

**CZWG Architects 1988**

# Crystal Palace Concert Platform

Like the fractured section of an alien spacecraft fallen to earth, the concert platform has lodged itself firmly in the grounds of Crystal Palace Park. It is as if on impact the vast shard of rusty steel had blasted a clearing in the trees and made a crater that became a lake and perfect seating bowl for 8000 people. In fact, the natural bowl already existed as a feature in the park as laid out by Joseph Paxton in 1864 when his Crystal Palace, designed for the Great Exhibition of 1851, was moved here from Hyde Park.

Far from being spaced-out, the sculptural gesture is informed by an understanding of the richness of the romantic English landscape within the park, the nineteenth-century notion of a folly (though these were usually neo-classical or neo-gothic in form) and the desire to make a thoroughly modern building that would be in harmony with the landscape. The architect identifies four principles that underlie the concept for the design: *natural colour* – the structure becomes an organic form through the patina of the untreated building materials which respond to the changing light and weather conditions; *gravitas* – permanence and belonging to the landscape expressed through the mass of a single material, Corten A steel; *levitas* – a lightness of composition that is sensitive to the landscape (the essential balance between the cantilevered acoustic reflector, the bulk of the accommodation module sitting on the concrete platform in the water and the monolithic speaker towers); and *simplicity* – a minimal intervention expressed in one continuous surface.

In winter the platform is empty and silent and the drawbridge at the back of the accommodation module is closed; in summer it is filled with performers, audiences and sound. The platform boasts the world's first outdoor application of an active acoustic system controlled through a computer processor, enabling the stage acoustic to be tuned to the atmos-

**Ian Ritchie Architects 1997**

**Ian Ritchie Architects 1997**

phere desired by the performers. A total of 46 speakers are concealed inside the shell. Thirty of them provide a special acoustic for an orchestra; the remaining 16 located at the top of the shell provide amplification to the front of the audience between the speaker columns. The columns house speakers and a 6000-watt sound-amplification system.

The platform demonstrates a successful marriage of design and specialist engineering, making a bold, elegant and useful addition to the park.

ADDRESS Crystal Palace Park (north-east corner), Sydenham Hill
CLIENT London Borough of Bromley
STRUCTURAL ENGINEER Atelier One
ACOUSTIC ENGINEER Paul Gilleiron Acoustic Design
CONTRACT VALUE £830,000
SIZE 23.5 metres wide (stage width); approximately 25 metres deep; acoustic canopy 11.34 metres high
BR Sydenham
ACCESS open for performances during the summer months

**Ian Ritchie Architects 1997**

# Camden and Islington

# J Sainsbury's Supermarket

The site, where the ABC Bakery once stood, is bounded by the Regent's Canal, Camden Street, Camden Road and Kentish Town Road. This mixed development, covering an entire block, comprises the supermarket, a crèche, small workshops, ten housing units, a bedsit flat and a one-bedroom maisonette.

The scale of the existing busy streets determined the size and proportions of the main Camden Road frontage – the bays are set out to mirror the widths of the listed Georgian houses opposite. The supermarket is based on a 'market-hall' structure – a column-free retail floor with a high, curved ceiling with a clear span of 43.2 metres. This is achieved by a central span supported by cantilevers which are in turn counterbalanced by tie-down rods. The open space allows for changes in retail methods, but at present it contains a devastatingly standard shop interior.

The structural form is revealed in the end elevations. Each element is designed to be functional, so there was close co-operation between the architect and the engineer, who often swapped roles, the architect calculating loads and inventing working parts and the engineer attempting to devise forms for the elements. As a result, both have tended to over-compensate for their efforts. Each joint is expressed as a separate part to help describe the process of construction.

It was possible for all the structural elements to be visible because of a new form of fire protection – an epoxy/ceramic material used previously on North Sea oil rigs but never before on a major building. It revolutionises the use of exposed steelwork and enhances Grimshaw's preoccupation with the role of architect/engineer. All façades are detailed in aluminium, steel and glass.

The cocoon-like aluminium-clad residential units sit along a 10-metre-wide strip parallel to the canal like loading bays for a ship. In order to

**Nicholas Grimshaw & Partners 1988**

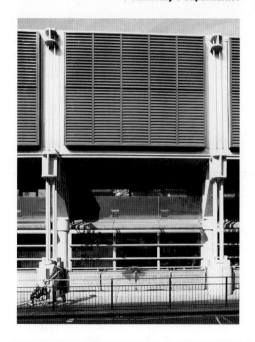

**Camden and Islington**

**Nicholas Grimshaw & Partners 1988**

exclude noise from the supermarket car park behind, a tall, open plan was devised, windowless at the back but top-lit and fronted by a north-facing double-height glazed wall incorporating a vertical sliding industrial door, which when opened allows the outdoors into the dining area of the house. The houses are built from concrete blockwork with felt-covered timber roofs and an external cladding of aluminium 'rainscreen' panels.

ADDRESS Camden Road, London NW1 [6H 45]
CLIENT J Sainsbury's plc
STRUCTURAL ENGINEER Kenchington Little & Partners
CONTRACT VALUE £15 million
SIZE OF SUPERMARKET 1300 square metres
TUBE Camden Town – Northern Line
ACCESS during shop-opening hours

**Nicholas Grimshaw & Partners 1988**

**Camden and Islington**

**Nicholas Grimshaw & Partners 1988**

# David Wild's House

No.44, Wild's own house, was completed first (built by himself with help from some of his students at the then South Bank Polytechnic) and was proposed as a prototype housing unit. Wild's idea of the home is based on a cave, which has private territory with cosy spaces at the back while its mouth gapes wide to let in light but is partially sheltered by trees. The architect says that he would not want to live in a glass box because he likes to feel safe and enclosed but at the same time wishes to have a view of the world around him. This primitive influence is reinforced by more recent architectural history, in particular the theories of Adolf Loos. Loos said: 'The building should be dumb on the outside and reveal its wealth only on the inside.' This is certainly true of No.44, where the large front window is set back from a flat, rendered façade, creating a discreet transition between house and street. Once inside, you enter a rich but uncluttered world of objects, paintings and colours, each with a personal story.

A reinforced-concrete frame cast *in situ* with precast-concrete floor planks and block infill forms the load-bearing shell structure which occupies two-thirds of the site. The gap down the right-hand side of the house allows light to reach inside from another angle (the stairs are located on this side) and leads into the back garden. The plan is a double square, 5.4 x 10.8 metres, with a 3.6-metre-square central space marked out by concrete columns which contains the hearth, the heart of the house. Behind the hearth a dog-leg stair, lined with bookcases, links all the floors. The ground floor accommodates children's bedrooms and the entrance; above this is the one-and-a-half-storey main living space at the front, with oak floors and white walls, and an open kitchen at the back. On a third storey is the master bedroom with the bathroom at the back, and a fourth studio floor leads on to an outdoor roof terrace.

The whole project is sited around a poplar tree in the front, which acts

**David Wild 1984, 1989**

**David Wild 1984, 1989**

as a foil for the corner concrete column of the façade and softens the hard lines of the interior space. Unfortunately, the original tree died after completion of the house, but another has been grown in its place. Another tragedy hit the house in 1987 when a mechanism in the hearth flue caused its chimney to catch fire, resulting in considerable damage to the stair core and to a lifetime's slide collection. It has been restored to its former state with only traces of black soot on book jackets to tell the tale. Thereafter, in the Japanese tradition, a small pond with running water was installed by the entrance to keep evil spirits at bay.

No.42, next door, was built to a brief for a client. The internal spaces are less intricate, with a double-height space on the first floor, a steel-framed mezzanine bedroom level at the back and a hearth at the centre following many of the same rules as No.44. A row of columns runs through the middle of the plan, a central column supporting a low-pitched roof. There are no outdoor terraces but the garden at the back is more accessible.

Both houses demonstrate an intelligent response to the past without copying its forms.

ADDRESS 42 and 44 Rochester Place, London NW1 [6G 45]
CLIENT David Wild
CONTRACT VALUE No.44 – £35,000; No.42 – £160,000
SIZE No.44 – 150 square metres; No.42 – 158 square metres,
TUBE Camden Town – Northern Line
ACCESS none

**David Wild 1984, 1989**

**Camden and Islington**

**David Wild 1984, 1989**

**One Off Studio and Showroom**

Ron Arad Associates (an architecture and design practice) and One Off Limited (a furniture workshop) moved into these courtyard premises while they were still a collection of derelict sheds and then designed and built the present showroom and offices around themselves.

Entering the showroom from the rusty fire-escape stairway is like walking into the belly of a whale and finding it full of swallowed treasure. To view Arad's gleaming steel furniture, you wander around the creaking landscaped timber floor, which scoops upwards at the back to make a hill, creating a division between the showroom and the office beyond. Space under the hill houses the air-handling unit for the air-conditioning bridge, which links the showroom to a small mezzanine at the back of the long shed. The office space is covered in a tensioned-fabric and expanded-metal shell structure (Expamet). The columns along the right-hand side not only support the roof but their calligraphic shapes (from the One Off alphabet) act as a radial track for the industrial PVC windows. The edges are stiffened with a sprung-steel frame so they can be fixed in any position along the curve of the column.

You can check out Arad's furniture and interior design in action at the two Belgo restaurants. The first is a few doors down on Chalk Farm Road while the latest sensation in providing fantastic cheap Belgian food for the masses is Belgo Central, in Covent Garden on the corner of Earlham and Shelton Streets.

ADDRESS 62 Chalk Farm Road, London NW1 [7E 44]
STRUCTURAL ENGINEER Neil Thomas at Atelier One
TUBE Chalk Farm – Northern Line
ACCESS to showroom

**Ron Arad/ Alison Brooks 1991**

**Ron Arad/ Alison Brooks 1991**

# Ambika Paul Children's Zoo
## London Zoo

The children's zoo houses domesticated animals from around the world and is intended as an educational facility for small children who may find it difficult to relate to animals isolated in large enclosures. Zoo staff and the architects met every week for eight months to determine what was required for the 40 different species and to establish a scale and plan that would be engaging and safe for children, parents and teachers.

The long thin site stretches from Sir Hugh Casson's Elephant House alongside the Grade 1-listed Penguin Pool by Tecton and Berthold Lubetkin. A series of paddocks connects three main buildings which face towards both the zoo and Regent's Park: the Courtyard Building, the Mess Building or Reindeer Den and the Camel and Llama Building. The architects' intention has been to respond to the domestic nature of the area's occupants and not to compete with the more powerful architectural expressions of neighbouring structures.

The main focus of the plan is the Courtyard Building, conceived as a traditional single-storey rough-pole barn enclosure with a corrugated-iron roof covering small pens. The corner of the courtyard is anchored by the Pet Care Centre: a taller, 8-metre-cubed building used as an educational study room and for static displays. The structure is a reinforced-block box with a roof lid resting on short timber posts on top of the walls and on four long poles within the space. It is lit through clerestory windows to create an atmosphere consistent with all the animal houses.

The Mess Building in the middle of the site next to the reindeer paddock is a refurbishment of a 1960s block to provide a paddock shelter. Reindeer happen to suffer from chronic dandruff so new ventilation was of utmost importance. A recycled-polypropylene slatted roof, based on military utility specifications, allows sufficient air circulation.

The Camel and Llama House is a tall pavilion at the end of the site.

**Wharmby Kozdon Architects 1995**

**Camden and Islington**

**Wharmby Kozdon Architects 1995**

Radial in plan to take in the extent of the paddock's long perimeter fence, it has load-bearing brick walls (sandy in colour) supporting a timber roof lined with moss. An arcade of timber poles supports deep overhanging eaves which shelter the animals' heads as they lean out of their stable.

The zoo's 'conservation in action' policy required that the sourcing of sustainable timber had to be in line with the World Wide Fund for Nature's guidelines (they recommend 50 per cent correct; here the architects achieved 90 per cent). Areas of timber cladding are made of English green oak and a tropical hardwood from managed forests in Papua New Guinea. To discourage birds and vermin from nesting in the barns, the depth of covered ledges was minimised and paper treated with boron used as insulation instead of glass fibre, which mice and rats enjoy.

The buildings are a triumph of environmentally sensitive construction techniques. However, the organisational model applied in all zoos is upheld: animals on the inside, humans on the outside. The Touch Paddock is an attempt to break the mould, though the cast-concrete, animal-shaped lumps adorned with push-button noises embedded in the dusty ground are a poor substitute for the real thing – the harassed goats and rabbits that lurk in the recesses of the small sheds and hutches.

ADDRESS Regent's Park, London W1 [2E 61]
CLIENT Zoological Society of London
STRUCTURAL ENGINEER Dewhurst Macfarlane & Partners
CONTRACT VALUE £780, 000
TUBE Great Portland Street – Circle, Hammersmith & City, Metropolitan Lines; Regent's Park – Bakerloo Line
ACCESS main zoo open 10.00–17.30 (last admission 16.30) daily

**Wharmby Kozdon Architects 1995**

Camden and Islington

**Camden and Islington**

**Wharmby Kozdon Architects 1995**

# Killick Street Residential Scheme

Many architects have specialised in extravagant luxury housing, but Avanti has become well known for small residential developments for housing trusts: the conversion and extension of a warehouse in Lambton Road, N19; offices and community housing in Endsleigh Gardens behind Euston Road; and a shared-ownership housing scheme in Boundary Road, NW8. The Killick Street scheme embraces a wider programme for urban regeneration in a tough area that for decades has been a haven for the less-than-sociable activities associated with King's Cross. It consists of 75 homes – 16 maisonettes and 59 flats – in five new blocks, and incorporates existing buildings (the General Picton pub and light-industrial warehouses) to create a more diverse mix of uses.

The rectangular site is bounded by All Saints Street, Killick Street, Wharfdale Road and New Wharf Road. Lavinia Grove – formerly a narrow cul-de-sac – has been extended by the architects to create a route through the site by adding a slim block of flats that fronts New Wharf Road. The rest of the site is conceived as a perimeter block with terraces of maisonettes and flats facing the streets on all four sides and gardens facing inwards to the centre.

All the larger, family homes are located on the ground floor and have their own gardens while most of the flats have balconies at the rear. As many homes as possible have their own external front door. All the blocks are four storeys and directly meet the pavement except for the block on Lavinia Grove, which is three storeys and set back to provide parking spaces on the narrow route and to maximise the distance between the flats and the light-industrial building opposite.

The scale and style of the architecture is vaguely consistent with the surrounding Victorian terraces – the architect describes the design as 'reinterpreting the tradition of the brick façade ... avoiding prettiness and

**Avanti Architects 1996**

pastiche' – so the acceptance of the Victorian terrace house as the model urban dwelling goes unchallenged, yet again. The interior plans may be well organised but they hide behind colourful elevations reminiscent of drawing-board graphics. And the deep layering of the frontages from pavement to front door obscures the means of access rather than facing up to the gritty urban context.

For the doctors' surgery on the Killick Street and Wharfdale Road corner of the site at the junction with Caledonian Road – originally designed as part of the scheme – the client (the Camden and Islington Family Health Services Authority) ended up using a design-and-build contract, so the Avanti design has been completely altered.

ADDRESS Killick Street, London N1 [2K 61]
CLIENT Peabody Trust, KUSH Housing Association
STRUCTURAL ENGINEER Dewhurst Macfarlane & Partners
CONTRACT VALUE £4.2 million
SIZE 1.2-hectare site
TUBE King's Cross – Circle, Hammersmith & City, Metropolitan, Northern, Piccadilly, Victoria Lines
ACCESS view from streets – no access to individual homes

**Avanti Architects 1996**

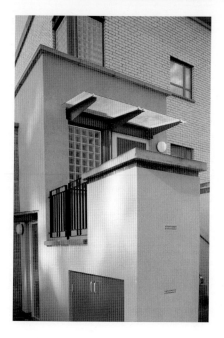

**Avanti Architects 1996**

**Camden and Islington**

**Private House**

This building represents one architect's concept of how a family home might operate and be occupied in the 1990s. It is a four-storey house built from scratch for approximately the same cost as buying a property of a similar size in the area. The result is not a gutted-interior-with-maintained-old-street-façade affair, but an open plan covering four storeys wrapped in a glass hood with rigorous attention to detail throughout, from the size of the letterbox to the type of glazing system employed. Each component illustrates changing patterns of living, with the flexibility to adapt to future requirements within the confines of a slow-moving, traditional street pattern.

The south-facing lot is protected front and back by mature trees and flanked by buildings of different scales and characters. Islington Borough Planning Department supported the design concept on condition that it did not impinge in any way on the neighbouring house, that the trees were retained and that the entire job was supervised by Future Systems alone to ensure that qualities of detailing and finish (particularly on the exterior) were not jeopardised.

The main construction is steel framed with concrete floor decks cast *in situ*. The front elevation is made of glass blocks (to maintain a degree of privacy) concealing a triple-height entrance hall. The rear of the house is a 50-degree slope of double-glazed Planar glass (with openable windows) allowing an unobstructed view from all floors into a sculpted garden. Shading from intense solar-heat gain on this side of the house is provided by the trees and white blinds fixed to the internal face of the glass. In the winter the house is passively heated by solar gain with additional heating provided by conventional radiators.

Any core services that require a modicum of privacy or simply need to be hidden away, such as bathrooms and storage, are housed in free-

**Camden and Islington**

**Future Systems 1994**

standing coloured units which float in unpartitioned floor spaces.

The range of materials and components used has been kept to a minimum – glass envelope, extruded aluminium sections as bracing, ceramic floor tiles. The absence of any skirting boards or architraves has resulted in precise treatment of how two finishes meet, often separated by a third in order to define the role and emphasise the quality of each finish.

This house is a landmark domestic building. Not only is it the first permanent structure to be built in London by this firm of architects but it challenged conventional planning regulations and a sensitive conservation area … successfully.

ADDRESS 40 Douglas Road, London N1 [7C 46]
CLIENTS Debra Hauer and Jeremy King
STRUCTURAL ENGINEER Anthony Hunt Associates
SIZE 215 square metres
TUBE Highbury and Islington – Victoria Line
ACCESS absolutely none; this is a private family home

**Future Systems 1994**

**Future Systems 1994**

**Sadler's Wells Theatre**

The first 'musick house' on this site was built in 1683 by Thomas Sadler and for five years acted as a side attraction to the medicinal well. The site's previous occupant before making way for the present theatre was designed in 1931 by F G M Chancellor with funds raised by Lilian Baylis as a north London home for her Old Vic Theatre Company. Once housing the Sadler's Wells Ballet, Sadler's Wells Opera and Sadler's Wells Royal Ballet (which moved out to become the Royal Ballet, 1946, English National Opera, 1968, and Birmingham Royal Ballet), the theatre – despite its cramped stage – has more recently maintained a year-round programme of dance, opera and lyric theatre.

The new building, completed using lottery funds, was designed to host touring companies, for commissioned new works of dance, opera and musical theatre and to nurture small companies over time. It now has a large performance stage (15 metres square) and a 26-metre-high flytower. But strict site boundaries and the retention of much of the existing steel-work of the circle seating determined that the overall scale remains largely unchanged.

The auditorium can vary its capacity from 900 to 1570 seats. The stage can be extended over the orchestra pit and the mesh panels covering four levels of gallery seating on the side walls can open to provide more seating or additional stage space, or close to be used as projection screens. The flying system (for scenery) is the first computerised system in the world and can drop a piece of flat scene from any one of its 75 bars at 1.8 metres per second to a dead stop.

The building brief emphasised the importance of taking an inclusive approach to access: disabled seating is the best in the house rather than stuck down in a corner at the front; textured floor surfaces, clear signage and generous corridor widths define main routes. The management is

**Arts Team @ RHWL with Nicholas Hare Architects 1998**

**Camden and Islington**

**Arts Team @ RHWL with Nicholas Hare Architects 1998**

particularly proud of the generous provision of ladies WCs to cope with the interval rush. The backstage area is open for educational purposes and training and incorporates a community centre for lectures, a rehearsal space and a courtyard café for artists and staff.

The new Sadler's Wells is also a building for the visual arts, with advisers from the Royal Academy of Arts and gallery-owner Sadie Coles to assist in curating the public areas. The glazed four-storey space that forms the main foyer (and primary means of public circulation) on Rosebery Avenue uses switchable glass as a polyvision screen wall: transparent during the day to reveal day-to-day activities, it is opaque at night so visitors and passers-by can watch a display of moving and still images, adverts and programming.

English Heritage indicated that the former Grade II-listed building was listed for its historical significance rather than its architectural merit. The new building shell remains as profoundly undistinguished. The performance areas and facilities have undoubtedly been improved and stage and performers penetrating the realms of the auditorium are a challenge for any set designer, choreographer or director. But a brick-clad concrete frame with slices of planar glazing inserted at faintly deconstructed angles, adorned with a polyvision screen for a high-tech glow, is far from meeting the brief's claim that: 'The underlying concept for the design is innovation.'

ADDRESS 179 Rosebery Avenue, London EC1 [3B 62]
STRUCTURAL ENGINEER Whitby & Bird
CONTRACT VALUE £30 million
TUBE Angel – Northern Line
ACCESS foyer open – guided tours available at a charge

**Arts Team @ RHWL with Nicholas Hare Architects 1998**

**Camden and Islington**

**Arts Team @ RHWL with Nicholas Hare Architects 1998**

**The British Library**

The story is a long one – what St John Wilson calls the 'Thirty Years War' in his recent book *The Design and Construction of the British Library*. The book gives a personal account of the life of the project from the first proposals to relocate the British Museum's library and department of prints and drawings to a site between Great Russell Street and Bloomsbury Way in 1951, through the commission (with Sir Leslie Martin, who withdrew soon after the appointment) in 1962 and the many changes in government which hampered progress, to breaking ground in 1984 (on an entirely different site), to the present day when we can breathe a huge sigh of relief and say that the new British Library is open – well, phase I of III at least.

The British Library was created by an Act of Parliament in 1972 when the decision was made to unite the newspaper collections, science and patents departments and the humanities collections to make a single national library. Accommodating the entire brief on the proposed site proved impossible, so in 1973 9 acres of vacant British Rail land in St Pancras were acquired for the project. The election of a Conservative government in 1979 and an increasing disgust for contemporary architecture led to a bitter attack on the project. But, as St John Wilson states: 'that the project has survived the onslaught … must surely be proof of its fundamental necessity.'

The design principles derive from the mid-nineteenth-century English Free School. This 'school of thought', promoted by such architects as Augustus Pugin, Alfred Waterhouse and George Edmund Street, was generated in response to the need for an increasing variety of public buildings. These architects took a functional approach, allowing each building to develop according to its particular needs and through a free gothic form rather than employing classical Orders and conventions. Sir George

**Colin St John Wilson and Partners 1997**

**Camden and Islington**

**Colin St John Wilson and Partners 1997**

Gilbert Scott's St Pancras Chambers (1867) next door is a superb example.

These principles determined a 'from inside out' design approach. So the fundamental task from the outset was to gain a full understanding of the library's workings and the needs and aspirations of its occupants – despite a brief which stated that the building must have a working life of 200–250 years. The conflicting requirements produced different spatial patterns according to different types of use: for instance, whether a reading room is visited for long or short periods determines whether natural daylight is admitted from above or via perimeter glazing and therefore how the book stacks and reading tables are arranged. The common denominator is a 7.8-metre grid of columns. There are five and a half basement levels (reaching a depth of 24.53 metres below ground) and nine levels above ground, with reading rooms on the upper floors and storage and general public areas on the lower and ground floors. Variations on the grid are introduced through the vertical dimension, where bays can rise from one to three storeys high.

The building holds approximately 50 million items (books, maps, manuscripts, music scores and patents). The shelving stretches for 340 kilometres. At least 6.25 million records are searchable on the Online Catalogue, forever increasing. Orders for the book stores can be placed automatically from the catalogue and are delivered via the Mechanical Book Handling System to your desk within 30 minutes.

The most astoundingly elegant of the building's features – the six-storey bronze and glass Miesian vault that holds the Kings Library (George III's collection of leather- and vellum-bound books) – embedded in the centre of the main hall for all to revere (particularly from the restaurant). The cascading terraced effect of the entrance hall is echoed inside

**Colin St John Wilson and Partners 1997**

Camden and Islington

**Colin St John Wilson and Partners 1997**

all the reading rooms on the west side, which are predominantly lit from above through clerestory windows and lantern lights. The side walls and floors of the entrance hall are of exposed brickwork (of the same stock in Leicestershire as St Pancras Chambers), a continuation of the external brickwork in the piazza. As one moves further into the building softer materials take over – travertine stone, polished brass, leather, American oak and carpeting.

The gulf between the sheer size of the building and the scale of its human users has been bridged by employing such devices as varied surfaces on which to sit, balconies on which to lean, short flights of steps and escalators, and visually breaking up large expanses of floor surface through a grid pattern in the stone and brick paving. Every detail from the readers' chairs to the book trolleys has been specially designed. All these factors have contributed to satisfy the fundamental requirement of any large public building – to make the public domain feel truly public.

ADDRESS 96 Euston Road, London NW1 [3J 61]
CLIENT The British Library Board
STRUCTURAL ENGINEER Ove Arup & Partners
SIZE total gross floor area 112,643 square metres
TUBE Euston – Northern, Victoria Lines; King's Cross – Circle, Hammersmith & City, Metropolitan, Northern, Piccadilly, Victoria Lines
ACCESS piazza, foyer, shop, exhibition rooms, café and restaurant open Monday and Wednesday to Friday 09.30–18.00; Tuesday 09.30–20.00; Saturday 09.30–17.00; Sunday 11.00–17.00

**Colin St John Wilson and Partners 1997**

**Camden and Islington**

**Colin St John Wilson and Partners 1997**

# Hampstead

**Surgery**

You could easily mistake this building for a Swiss chalet when in fact it is a new general-practice surgery, on the site of the old surgery and adjoining car park. In order to maintain the precious parking space, the building evolved from the use of Vierendeel beams, which span the car-park deck in one gesture, squatting on low, stumpy concrete columns.

The structure had to be low cost and low maintenance, hence the use of largely prefabricated building parts: a steel main frame with precast-concrete plank floors, unpainted timber weather-boarding on exterior walls, and a roof made of a sandwich of galvanised aluminium and layers of insulation. The curved roof seems to slide out to the sides like wings unfolding, but is held in place on each side by v-shaped brackets. Inside, the sliding-roof effect has created a barrel vault, the highest point (containing skylights) covering the waiting room at the centre of the plan. Tensile sails make the walls of the waiting area, separating it from the corridor to the offices and consulting rooms which run around the perimeter of the building. The surgery is unmistakeable from the outside, especially because of the distinctive perforated-steel ramp and the way the building provides a contrasting footing for the tower block.

ADDRESS 111 Adelaide Road, London NW3 [7B 44]
CLIENT Drs M D Peters, Frances A Loughridge, W J Clayton, I K Sienkowski
STRUCTURAL ENGINEER David Powell Edmondson & Partners
CONTRACT VALUE £610,421
SIZE 476 square metres
TUBE Chalk Farm – Northern Line
ACCESS surgery hours

Hampstead

**Pentarch Architects 1992**

**Pentarch Architects 1992**

# Lisson Gallery

The Lisson Gallery is like a section of the street stripped bare. Each of its four storeys strictly corresponds in height to those of the neighbouring buildings. But the façades of the ground- and first-floor galleries have been peeled away to reveal the guts of the building through floor-to-ceiling-height square glass panels which can slide back to enable large works to be moved in and out of the gallery. The second and third storeys are occupied by flats with sheer concrete façades to allow some privacy from the school playground across the street.

Each of the basement, ground and first floors provides a 7-metre-squared space linked to the others by an atelier-type stairway to the side. This arrangement allows smaller shows to be exhibited in a single space or for full retrospectives to flow around the entire building. The route begins in the side entrance of the old Lisson Gallery on Lisson Street, which is linked to the new space by a long reception corridor. The journey becomes a succession of discoveries, exiting on to the adjacent Bell Street. This 'possession of the space by the visitor', as Fretton calls it, makes the gallery an integral part of a varied community, helping to break down the prejudices on which many art galleries thrive.

ADDRESS 52 Bell Street, London NW1 [5C 60]
CLIENT Lisson Gallery London Limited
STRUCTURAL ENGINEER Price & Myers
CONTRACT VALUE £500,000 approximately
TUBE Edgware Road – Circle, District, Hammersmith & City Lines
ACCESS open Monday to Friday, 10.00–18.00; Saturday 10.00–13.00

**Hampstead**

**Tony Fretton Architects 1990**

**Tony Fretton Architects 1990**

# Grand Stand
## Lord's Cricket Ground

Lord's Cricket Ground has seen a succession of pavilions since the first one-room building was erected c 1820 (it burned down five years later during a Harrow v Winchester match). Today the ground is surrounded by seven pavilions (or stands), the oldest of which is Thomas Verity's Pavilion (1899–90) on the west side, flanked by the Allen and Warner corner stands (1958). The Tavern Stand (1966) sits next to Hopkins' Mound Stand (1987, see page 196) on the south side and the Edrich and Compton Stands (1991) make up the east side of the ground. The most recent addition, the Grand Stand, now occupies the north side, replacing a stand built in 1926 and increasing its seating capacity by more than 50 per cent to 6200 (the overall ground capacity is 30,500).

Verity's Pavilion and Hopkins' Mound Stand at last have a new architectural rival. The canopy of pith helmets that distinguishes the Mound Stand, responding sympathetically to Verity's colonial-style pavilion, now faces a sleek, streamlined construction which respects the scale of its surroundings, though it has a taller flagpole. It is therefore appropriate that the central flagpole should appear to be the *raison d'être* of the structure. Three columns support a two-storey high spine beam, which in turn supports the upper tier. All vertical circulation is at the rear. Staircases are cantilevered out to form a canopy between the building and the screen of trees at the boundary of the site. An aerofoil roof incorporating motorised blinds shades the upper tier. Private boxes have front and rear glazing (opaque at the back for privacy), allowing glimpses of the trees behind and reducing the bulk of this, the largest single stand in the ground.

Most of the elements are self-finished (for instance, diamond-plate steel stair treads and polished precast-concrete floor and ceiling slabs) or painted white to enhance the lightness of the structure. The high degree of prefabrication used to control quality and for efficiency during the tight

**Nicholas Grimshaw & Partners 1998**

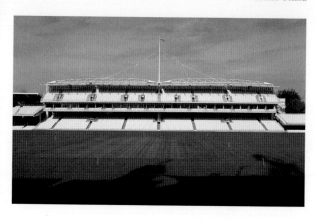

**Nicholas Grimshaw & Partners 1998**

construction schedules (over two closed seasons) is reflected in the graceful composition of the building, which seems to have been lowered on to the ground rather than built up from it, appearing to hinge and unfold from the central column.

ADDRESS St John's Wood Road, London NW8 [4B 60]
CLIENT Marylebone Cricket Club
STRUCTURAL ENGINEER Ove Arup & Partners
CONTRACT VALUE £12 million
SIZE 6760 square metres on a 2160 square-metre footprint
TUBE St John's Wood – Jubilee Line
ACCESS for information on tours call 0171 432 1033/289

**Nicholas Grimshaw & Partners 1998**

# Mound Stand
### Lord's Cricket Ground

At the end of the 1980s several architectural journals nominated this project as the 'best' building of the decade. Perhaps this is because it incorporated so many different types of building technique: the restoration and completion of the existing brick arcade built by Thomas and Frank Verity in 1898 at ground level, the cantilevered steel-framed decks above, and the tent structure of the roof. These involve three diverse technologies, all executed with the utmost precision. Each layer of the stand is clearly visible from St John's Wood Road, so the construction can be logically understood. There are no disguises.

The Marylebone Cricket Club, in its stubbornly traditional way, still distinguishes between types of spectator. This in turn informed Hopkins' design. The general public sit in the terraces on the lowest level, box proprietors on a cantilevered promenade (all the boxes are in corporate ownership except one belonging to Paul Getty, Junior, who funded half of the project); members and debenture holders have access to an open upper promenade beneath the fabric roof – 4500 spectators in all. The atmosphere on the top deck harks back to the quintessentially British scene of a marquee pitched on a village green with spectators scoffing cucumber sandwiches and sipping cups of tea.

The structure that supports the PVC-coated fabric roof is strongly reminiscent of the rigging on a boat – six vertical masts and a series of projecting steel booms with steel cables that tie down into concrete piles at the back of the stand and on to the front of the cantilevered promenade to achieve overall stability. The superstructure of the cantilevered promenade and boxes was determined by the need to use thin columns that would not obscure the view on to the pitch from the terraces. A spine girder runs along the centre of the plan supported by hollow columns (with masts for the roof slotted inside) set every 18.3 metres along the

**Michael Hopkins & Partners 1985–1987**

Hampstead

**Michael Hopkins & Partners 1985–1987**

terrace. Tapered girders cantilever on either side of the spine, like ribs, to hold a metal deck and a 160-mm concrete slab for seating and enclosures at the rear. The boxes have an appropriately old-school changing-room feel to them, with fairfaced-blockwork walls and simple glazed doors that fold back to frame the pitch. On the same level but overlooking St John's Wood Road there are private dining rooms and lavatories enclosed by glass bricks to admit light while obscuring the activities within from passers-by.

One of the pleasures of the building is that there was no need to insulate it or to make the decks watertight as it is only fully occupied on eight fair-weather days of the year. If it should rain, terrace spectators can shelter under the huge Verity arches and have a drink at one of the bars while members and their guests promenade on the top deck.

(On-site at the time of writing is the new Media Centre by Future Systems, pictured opposite.)

ADDRESS St John's Wood Road, London NW8 [4B 60]
CLIENT Marylebone Cricket Club
STRUCTURAL ENGINEER Ove Arup & Partners
TUBE St John's Wood – Jubilee Line
ACCESS seasonal

**Michael Hopkins & Partners 1985–1987**

**Hampstead**

**Michael Hopkins & Partners 1985–1987**

# MCC Indoor Cricket School

The MCC Indoor Cricket School provides opportunities for players of all ages and abilities to learn and enjoy cricket. The aspects of 'learning' and 'enjoying' are expressed in the 'double-sided pavilion' plan: the clubhouse area or pavilion is integrated into the front of the steel-columned training building affording sheltered views of the school on its south side and overlooking the Nursery Ground (practice ground) to the north. The three-storey height of the training building is determined by the pavilion, which accommodates offices on the ground floor, a bar on the first and a function room on the second with a detachable north-facing tarpaulin façade to take advantage of views of practice matches.

Two features were identified as important for an ideal indoor facility: the quality of light and the floor surface. The floor is a concrete slab lined in a specialist surface called Uni-Turf Vinyl Sheet. The barrel-vaulted roof relates to the module of nets below and incorporates these into its structure. A system of partial glazing on the east-facing side of each vault combined with swathes of fabric-louvered blinds diffuses direct sunlight. The roof structure also provides a means of support for additional lighting to be used in the evenings. The building is unostentatious in appearance and straightforward in plan (it took only ten months to build), complementing the variety of designs of the stands in the main ground nearby (see pages 196 and 192).

ADDRESS St John's Wood Road, London NW8 [4B 60]
STRUCTURAL ENGINEER Price & Myers
CONTRACT VALUE £2 million
SIZE 2405 square metres
TUBE St John's Wood – Jubilee Line
ACCESS for information on tours call 0171 432 1033/289 1611

**David Morley Architects 1995**

Hampstead

Hampstead

**David Morley Architects 1995**

# Mill Lane Gardening Project

In 1962 Walter Segal was confronted with the problem of providing temporary accommodation for his family while their house was being rebuilt. At a materials cost of £800 (£6500 today) and completed in two weeks, the first Segal self-build 80-square-metre house still stands in the garden of the Highgate house. The key to the success of the building was the rigorous simplification of the construction process: one person with basic carpentry skills could carry out the work (with perhaps the exception of services and roofing). Segal's system is based on a modular grid determined by the sizes of standard materials – ideally these could be disassembled and resold. The frame is timber, clad in woodwool and faced with roofing felt on the exterior and chipboard waste paper inside. The roof is flat (avoiding the use of scaffolding), surfaced with felt and held down by bricks and 35mm of water. Over 30 years later, the building would still pass tests for water penetration or structural failure. Details such as using stainless- rather than mild-steel bolts and timber jointing rather than nail-plate joints (too much movement) have been adopted by many subsequent schemes.

Five per cent of new housing stock in Great Britain is accounted for by self-build – the figure would be far greater if the political establishment could learn to appreciate the method's merits. Homes can be built for about one-third of usual cost. The Walter Segal Self-Build Trust was set up in 1988 to continue Segal's work after his death in 1985. The trust's aim is to help people with limited means to build themselves homes or community projects such as Mill Lane. What was intended as temporary accommodation has developed into forms of permanent housing where families can build their own environments from start to finish, led by their own programme and with the ability to extend and change it as they wish.

The Mill Lane Gardening Project is a centre for adults with learning

**Hampstead**

**Simon Yauner Architects 1992**

**Simon Yauner Architects 1992**

difficulties. The land is owned by Camden Council but had been deserted for years. A corner of the site was allocated to CSMH for a gardening project. By the end of 1992 the trainees and a number of volunteers had aquired more than just green fingers. The building of the centre was carried out by the users themselves so that the construction process became an integral part of their training. Simon Yauner and his engineer, Rene Weisner, developed the design: discontinuous construction allowing movement between layers. Stephen Backes, a carpenter and welder, was employed to supervise the site and train the volunteers and trainees in basic building skills. Electrical and plumbing works were sub-contracted.

This seems to have been a rewarding process for everyone involved. The method opens a door on an architectural philosophy which isn't about monumentality; trainees gained confidence and learned skills (being prompt was high on Backes' agenda) which opened another door labelled 'anything is possible' ... as long as you turn up on time!

For details of other current schemes, contact The Walter Segal Self-Build Trust, 57 Chalton Street, London NW1 (0171–388 9582).

ADDRESS 160 Mill Lane, London NW6 [5H 43]
CLIENT Camden Society for People with Learning Difficulties (CSMH)
STRUCTURAL ENGINEER Trigram Partnership
CONTRACT VALUE £70,400 (excluding architect's and engineer's fees)
SIZE 169 square metres
TUBE Kilburn – Jubilee Line
ACCESS open (but introduce yourself to whoever is around when you arrive)

Hampstead

**Simon Yauner Architects 1992**

**Simon Yauner Architects 1992**

**Sarum Hall School**

Domestic in its outward appearance, this primary school sits comfortably on a quiet leafy street. On the one hand it's not unlike one of its grand, detached-house neighbours, but on the other it's a bit of an outbuilding compared with the sturdy red-brick Arts and Crafts fire station opposite.

The most challenging aspect of any school is the plan – deciding how to organise the activities that take place so as to create a stimulating environment which can be easily supervised. Here the headmistress' office is located in the long north-facing building at the front on Eton Avenue in a pivotal location between the communal areas: the front entrance, the entrance hall, a double-height school hall/gymnasium and a dining hall. The entrance hall leads into the classroom wing which runs due south at a right angle to the front wing. The two wings form a protective enclosure around the playground. Science and art rooms have been given equal and prominent status, on the second floor of the front wing, taking full advantage of the height of the exposed timber-trussed roof structure punctured by an oversized dormer window and rooflights to maximise daylight.

Given the calm suburban surroundings and the sympathetic complexion of the two-storey, barn-like construction with its steep-pitched slate roof, it is somewhat distracting that the architects describe the project in terms of an architectural language of layering: a fleshy external layer of brick (to please the planners) surrounding a white inner-sanctum building (satisfying the client). This is a language of aesthetics rather than of construction and were it not for a restrained palette of materials and the precise execution of the detailing, the concept may not have undergone such a satisfactory translation. It is a mature and confident building but is slightly lacking in charisma in this respect. As Anthony McIntyre explains, as he assesses the building for *Architecture*

**Allies & Morrison 1995**

Allies & Morrison 1995

Hampstead

*Today*, 'I am really arguing for the development of a method; with an even deeper consideration of the "layers" themselves and a more playful attitude towards their assembly, this could become a strong theoretical and practical method.' The architects are on their way to developing a modern vernacular which makes for a secure and intimate environment.

ADDRESS Eton Avenue, London NW3 [7B 44]
CLIENT Sarum Hall School Trust Limited
STRUCTURAL ENGINEER Price & Myers
SIZE 1442 square metres
TUBE Swiss Cottage – Jubilee Line
ACCESS request permission before entering

Hampstead

**Allies & Morrison 1995**

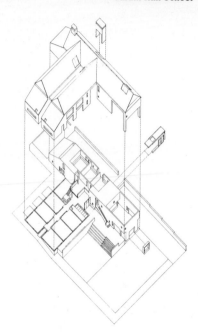

**Hampstead**

**Allies & Morrison 1995**

# From the City to Stansted

**City House**

CZWG are well known for creating bold imagery, taking themes from the site and the personality of the occupant and reflecting these in the plan and use of materials. The basic construction here is straightforward and economical: brick with standard concrete floors. The external themes seem to be a mixture of Scottish baronial (cast-concrete log lintels), French château (part mansard roof) and screens like the sails of a boat.

Inside, there are plain plaster walls (which get lighter as you progress up the four levels) and ceilings left bare to expose the floor slabs. The top-floor studio is lined with unpainted chipboard, which has a glowing, natural colour and provides insulation. A basic rectangular shell is countermanded by the internal plan, which is based around a circular geometry dictated by a curving staircase that runs around the perimeter. This arrangement creates a large sweeping space (the bedroom on the first floor), or a space like a castle ante-chamber for the dining room leading on to the main living room on the second floor.

The most publicised aspect of the house must be the kitchen, where the wall surfaces reveal their stud partitioning – a pioneering example of the distressed look, a theme which cropped up in many interior landmarks of the 1980s. With a terrace outside the studio on the top floor, it goes to show that in England, every media person's home could be not only their castle, but their playground too.

ADDRESS Britton Street, London EC1 [4B 62]
SIZE 350 square metres
TUBE Farringdon – Circle, Metropolitan Lines
ACCESS none

**From the City to Stansted**

**CZWG Architects 1986–1988**

**CZWG Architects 1986–1988**

# Clerkenwell Green House/Flats/Offices

There are few architectural offices in London that can truly be said to be practising the art and science of architecture. Paxton Locher is one. They have confidently demonstrated that they can take a thoroughly innovative approach to functional requirements alongside a pleasure in creating space. The fact that the husband-and-wife team started out by converting warehouses into homes and offices for their own use has enabled them to experiment and this in turn has attracted more visionary clients.

This site was originally found by Paxton Locher for the Jerwood Foundation (see page 118), but the conditions could not take the brief. Reluctant to let it go to waste, the architects embarked on their first new-build project in the city, comprising a three-bedroom house and offices for themselves and four apartments. Paxton Locher enjoy a thoroughly urban environment, and this has all the essential qualities: a deep, narrow plot confined by party walls at either side, lacking much natural light, and hindered by long escape-route distances and a petrol garage in the backyard.

The box of tricks and devices employed in the final plan was arrived at through an exhaustive process of research and experimentation. The seven-storey front section has the offices at ground and basement levels and five floors of apartments above. The introduction of a covered alleyway through the middle of the site enabled secure independent access by a bespoke spiral staircase to the apartments and outdoor access to the three-storey house at the rear (the discovery of traces of medieval clay and chalk at the rear of the site which had to remain untouched reduced the size of this area considerably). The 16-metre-long passage ending in a timber bridge across a moat (both calming and light reflective) creates

**Paxton Locher Architects 1997**

**Paxton Locher Architects 1997**

an uplifting transition between the architects' offices and home.

Now confined on all four sides, the house could only be penetrated by natural light through the roof. So the plan is based on the idea of a Roman atrium, with a retractable glass roof over the kitchen and dining area exposing the heart of the building to the elements. The main bedroom and playroom, located on mezzanine floors on either side of the dining area, are connected by a glass-walled bridge. The bridge becomes a corridor to the back of the building and another block containing two rooms for the children and a roof terrace.

The catalogue of details is endlessly and elegantly inventive: the mezzanine balustrade screens made from cafetière mesh; the simple sliding mechanisms for the apartment windows placed on the outside of the building, thus contributing to the composition of the front elevation; the creeper on the double-height dining-room wall that adds natural colour and texture to a substantially white interior.

To say the interior is a dazzlingly tranquil oasis is an understatement – to attain such saturation of light in London is a miracle.

ADDRESS 8–9 Clerkenwell Green, London EC1 [4B 62]
CLIENT Paxton Locher
STRUCTURAL ENGINEER Elliott Wood Partnership
CONTRACT VALUE £621 per square metre
SIZE approximately 225 square metres
TUBE Farringdon – Circle, Hammersmith & City, Metropolitan Lines
ACCESS although the offices are on the ground floor, please respect the fact that the rest of the site is occupied by private homes and not on general view to the public

**From the City to Stansted**

**Paxton Locher Architects 1997**

**From the City to Stansted**

**Paxton Locher Architects 1997**

# Minster Court

The seat of the London Underwriting Centre, Minster Court, has been dubbed 'Munster Court', making a more-than-suitable set for the 1960s spoof-horror television series. This gothic chocolate cake comprises three steel-framed blocks merged into one by a curtain wall whose surface constantly changes direction to form icing peaks and mock buttresses. The granite panels are 7.5 metres wide by a full storey high and were transported on specially adapted trucks that could cope with their size. The ground-floor slab was made considerably more substantial so vehicles could drive into the centre of the building during construction to speed up the process. Toilet pods were designed by Mitsubishi.

There is 50 per cent more space here than in the Lloyd's building (see page 220), arranged around a central atrium. Horrifyingly, in August 1991 one of the three buildings went up in smoke, causing £120 million worth of damage. The fire started at the base of the atrium then spread rapidly; the escalators were wrapped in sterling board which encouraged the fire considerably. The accident was blamed on debris left around the site, prompting attention to the installation of fire protection earlier in the construction process.

ADDRESS Mark Lane, London EC3 [7E 62]
CLIENT Prudential Portfolio Managers
CONTRACT VALUE £178 million
SIZE 59,000 square metres
TUBE Tower Hill – Circle, District Lines
ACCESS none

**GMW Partnership 1988–1991**

**GMW Partnership 1988–1991**

**Lloyd's of London**

This is not a tower block – it is rarely perceived as a whole at any one time. Rather, one glimpses bits of gleaming stainless steel, or electric-blue light at night, patched on to the sober City landscape. More like a vertical street, its close proximity to other buildings allows it physically to penetrate its surroundings. The unusual configuration is a result of its location within the irregular medieval street pattern and the dominant philosophy of the architect that the building should appear to be assembled from a 'kit of parts'.

The main structure is remarkably simple in plan: a stack of 'o' ring floors (varying in level from six to 12 storeys) carried on central concrete columns and braced external columns creates a support for the vast tubular-steel lattice framework of the 70-metre-high central atrium. Six precast-concrete satellite service towers cling, structurally independent, to the exterior of the main frame; the lavatory modules plugged into the sides can feasibly be replaced. The tower is surmounted by five stunning electric-blue cranes. All the structural details are fully on display, giving the viewer an understanding of just how the building is supported and braced.

Inside, the atmosphere is awesomely cathedral-like. The whole point of the Lloyd's building is to house one of the world's most famous financial institutions, so the focus for activities is the underwriting room (the Room) on the ground floor and first three mezzanine levels. 'Boxes' are provided on each floor – these are flexible work terminals containing storage units, worktops, VDUs, telephones, and so on – to be rented by the underwriters. The boxes were developed as kits by Tecno. This type of open-plan, flexible, fully-serviced space is called an 'omniplatz'. Light pours down into the canyon-like atrium space and additional light comes from large fittings, which also act as air extractors, set into the ceiling.

**Richard Rogers Partnership 1978–1986**

**Richard Rogers Partnership 1978–1986**

The triple-glazed external cladding skin acts as an air duct from ceiling to floor.

With enough stainless steel to make 20,000 sinks, ducting and pipes that could stretch from London to Brighton, floor space to cover seven football pitches, and unique and thorough detailing (many parts performing more than one task), this building is functionally and aesthetically a living and breathing machine.

ADDRESS Lime Street, London EC3 [7E 62]
CLIENT Corporation of Lloyd's of London
STRUCTURAL ENGINEER Ove Arup & Partners
CONTRACT VALUE £169 million
SIZE 47,000 square metres
TUBE Monument – Circle, District Lines
ACCESS only by booking in advance; telephone 0171–623 7100

**Richard Rogers Partnership 1978–1986**

**Bracken House**

The original Bracken House was the Grade II-listed home of the *Financial Times* (its the pink stone echoing the paper's distinctive pink newsprint), built by Sir Albert Richardson in 1959. The dispersal of the newspaper industry to developing areas such as Docklands throughout the 1980s left many valuable sites in the City empty, to be converted into London bases for American and Japanese merchant banks. The old *FT* building had two office-block wings linked by an unspectacular octagonal print-works in the centre. It was this central part that Hopkins demolished and readdressed.

A new oval plan has been sandwiched between the old wings. None of the old building was at right angles to the site, whereas the Hopkins doughnut has been set parallel to Friday Street so it bulges out as if being squeezed in a clamp. The plan is centred on a rectangular atrium containing lifts with glass-pavement brick walkways all around to allow light to filter into the office floors. The four corners are marked by hollow, wedge-shaped columns which house services. The six floors are concrete on metal decking, the thickness being kept to a minimum to reduce the total height of the building to conform with the height restrictions imposed by the proximity of St Paul's Cathedral.

Each floor is open plan with a 4-metre-deep rim around the edge marked by secondary columns to allow for partitioning or private spaces. This rim is crucial to the nature of the façade. Hopkins' belief is that architectural form is based on structure. The brief here was that the façade should be long-life, low maintenance and structural and should refer to the materials of the old building. Load-bearing piers are of solid Hollington stone (sandstone used in Richardson's building). The bay-window panels rest on huge three-armed brackets, also load-bearing, made of gun-metal (bronze, zinc and lead), a structural material. In the

**Michael Hopkins & Partners 1989–1991**

**Michael Hopkins & Partners 1989–1991**

event of a fire the floor beams in the 4-metre span act as cantilevers so no added fire protection was required, hence the exposed material on the outside. Ceiling fixing plates on the inside indicate where brackets connect the outside structure to the inside floor slabs.

Bracken House is technically very creative and materials have been tested beyond decorative roles, but on the face of it, it is heavy and rather dreary. Not only is it squeezed from the sides, but St Paul's has squashed it with its big foot too.

ADDRESS 1 Friday Street, London EC4 [7C 62]
CLIENT Obayashi Europe
BY: Harakazu Nakamua
STRUCTURAL ENGINEER Ove Arup & Partners
TUBE Mansion House – Circle, District Lines
ACCESS none

**Michael Hopkins & Partners 1989–1991**

**Michael Hopkins & Partners 1989–1991**

**Milton Gate**

This is the commercial-building debut of one of the most distinguished British architects. Sir Denys Lasdun's career is characterised by such projects as the apartments at 26 St James's Place, SW1 (1958), the Royal College of Physicians near Regent's Park (early 1960s) and the National Theatre on the South Bank (1969). These works are grounded in a sense of social responsibility, designed at a time when a building opportunity offered the potential for architectural experimentation with the will to enhance society. Now architects are at the mercy of construction techniques and predatory clients. Symbols borrowed from other eras pinned to steel frames replace responses to specific environmental problems.

Here the metaphor is 'the castle' (borrowed from the nearby Barbican and Lasdun's interest in Charles Rennie Mackintosh), but unlike other fortress-offices nearby (with wretched granite walls and impervious mirrored glass) Milton Gate is a modest, watery stronghold. A partially visible grid frame is veiled in blue-green glass, giving a semi-transparent and occasionally rippled effect. The double skin provides a space between the glass and frame for maintenance walkways and reduces solar gain and heat loss. The interior is based around a central courtyard and moated elevator tower with walkways overhead linking the offices around the sides.

ADDRESS Chiswell Street, London EC2 [5D 62]
CLIENT Land Securities
SIZE 19,700 square metres
TUBE Barbican – Circle, District Lines (through Beech Street tunnel)
ACCESS none

From the City to Stansted

**Denys Lasdun Peter Softley & Associates 1990**

**Denys Lasdun Peter Softley & Associates 1990**

# The Helicon

The brief was to design a 'modern steel and glass landmark building for a corner City block to combine retail and office space that is both energy efficient and economical to run.' Not an unusual office-block development perhaps, but this site was purchased when the property market was at its lowest point during the early 1990s, making it one of the shrewder developments in the City. Competitively priced tenders from builders were secured at this point, when there was no other work around, and a bluechip tenant (Marks & Spencer) signed up.

The plan is arranged around four stair and lift towers, noticeable because of their curved ends which protrude from the front and rear elevations. Eleven storeys in all (two below ground level) are stepped up and around the towers. The overhangs, recesses and changes of angle which animate the elevations also create a distinction between the retail and office spaces. A planar, glazed entrance announces Marks & Spencer (which occupies the bottom five storeys) within a triple-height frontage on Moorgate that reflects the triple-height volume of the store's interior. A separate double-height glazed entrance serves the offices on the south-west corner of the site facing both Moorgate and South Place. Project architect Graham Anthony formerly worked for Richard Rogers Partnership, which explains why the suspended, curved, steel and glass office façade is influenced by the glass curtain at the Channel 4 building (see page 78).

At the heart of the office floors is an atrium with its base at third-floor level (located above the retail space). This, along with the use of clear, untinted glass, maximises the admission of natural daylight. At one end of the atrium the office floors are stepped back to form a series of balconies planted with semi-mature trees. The desire for maximum transparency led to the use of a triple-glazed cladding system incorporating a 900-

**Sheppard Robson Architects 1996**

**Sheppard Robson Architects 1996**

mm void to deal with solar gain and glare control. The system is not unlike that used at the Lloyd's building (see page 220), where openings at the top and bottom of the glazing allow air to flow through for cooling in summer and are shut off to act as a thermal buffer in winter. Similarly, air here is extracted through light fittings and drawn across chilled water panels fixed within the suspended ceiling for additional cooling. Also contained within the glazing void are maintenance walkways and automatically adjustable louvre blinds pitched at such an angle that occupants have an uninterrupted view out whether sitting or standing.

The Helicon is an example of the recent move towards a more streamlined office building, less concerned to stand out from the crowd, and more about considering the needs of its occupants by providing environmental conditions and mixed use of floor space and about integrating itself into the streetscape through the manipulation of mass and extensive use of clear glass. Although the architectural form lacks the confidence of the more outstanding City developments, such as the Lloyd's building and Bracken House (see page 224), the Helicon has adopted many of their features and signals a promising departure from the granite-clad cartoon castles of the 1980s.

ADDRESS 1 South Place/Moorgate, London EC2 [5D 62]
CLIENT London & Manchester Property Asset Management
STRUCTURAL ENGINEER John Savage Associates
SIZE 22,100 square metres
TUBE Moorgate – Circle, Hammersmith & City, Metropolitan, Northern Lines
ACCESS to retail area only

**Sheppard Robson Architects 1996**

**Sheppard Robson Architects 1996**

**Tower Bridge Visitors' Facilities**

The building forms an entrance to a new exhibition redesigned in 1994 to commemorate the centenary of the construction of Tower Bridge. Completion of the entrance pavilion had to coincide with the opening of the exhibition. In order to speed things along, a design-and-build contract was employed before Michael Squire Associates was appointed to complete the job and to proceed with the design and construction of a new restaurant on the south side of the bridge.

The visitors' pavilion provides an enclosure for a ticket office and staff facilities. The main structure consists of two central beams which carry lateral beams cantilevered to the perimeter then held down with tie rods. The orientation of the building and its glazed walls take full advantage of the river views as it wraps itself around the existing curved parapet wall. Terrazzo panels replace glass to form an enclosure on the south side for staff quarters.

The new structure has adopted an appearance more akin to the fine tracery that decorates the bridge than to its heavy granite piers. A contemporary frill.

ADDRESS north side of Tower Bridge [F1 79]
CLIENT Corporation of London
CONTRACT VALUE £230,000
TUBE Tower Hill – Circle, District Lines
ACCESS open 10.00–17.15 daily

**Michael Squire Associates 1993**

**Michael Squire Associates 1993**

# No.1 Poultry

Poultry is named after the poulterers who used to live here before the street was demolished in 1817 because of the filth and stench that emanated from the local prison. No.1 lies at the confluence of eight streets that lead to Sir John Soane's Bank of England (1788–1808). Other distinguished neighbours include Sir Edwin Lutyens' Midland Bank Head Office (1924–39) on the opposite side of the street, Sir Edwin Cooper's National Westminster Bank (1930–32) on the corner of Poultry and Princes Street, and the Mansion House (1739–52) on Walbrook designed by George Dance the Elder as the official residence of the Lord Mayor.

The site was formerly occupied by the Mappin & Webb building (1870) designed by J & J Belcher in the high-Victorian neo-Gothic style. In the late 1960s property developer Peter Palumbo submitted plans to demolish the building and replace it with a 1967 design for a modernist steel and glass tower surrounded by a pedestrian plaza by Mies van der Rohe. The proposal was refused planning permission by the then Secretary of State, though this did not 'rule out redevelopment of the site if there was an acceptable proposal for replacing existing buildings.'

Proposals were revived in 1985. Mies had since died, and James Stirling Michael Wilford & Associates, having recently completed what has since become a post-modern icon – the celebrated Staatsgalerie in Stuttgart (1977–82) – were commissioned to work on a new scheme containing offices, shops and public spaces. In 1988 a scheme was approved, followed by over two years of legal argument and soothing of public emotions over the proposed demolition of seven listed buildings. Construction finally began in 1994.

In true post-modern style, Stirling's building adheres to the existing street pattern and incorporates symbolic references to surrounding buildings, while the winged clock tower harks back to the Mappin & Webb

**James Stirling Michael Wilford & Associates**

**James Stirling Michael Wilford & Associates**

building's circular turret. Construction techniques are also post-modern: a thin veneer of sandstone and granite clipped to a steel frame with a *Play-school* palette of colours applied to window frames and balustrades.

There are shops at basement and ground-floor levels and a pedestrian passage punctures the plan, linking shopping colonnades on the two main street frontages with an open courtyard at the centre which provides access to Bank Underground. The courtyard void, circular at ground- and first-floor levels, becomes a triangle when surrounded by the upper office floors, which are surmounted by a roof garden and restaurant.

Completion of truly significant buildings in London, for instance the British Library (see page 180), is often so prolonged that they become a crystallisation of the moment when the first notion of their being hit the drawing board. This makes it difficult to compare them with other buildings – it's rather like comparing cave paintings with graffiti without taking into account the evolution in between. Ultimately No.1 Poultry is London's post-modern flagship, designed by one of the world's leading proponents of that style. Today we can be happy for its contribution to the texture of our architectural heritage, though back in the 1980s one might have cast a more sceptical eye.

ADDRESS 1 Poultry, London EC2 [6D 62]
CLIENT City Acre Property Investment Trust & Alstadtbau Limited
STRUCTURAL ENGINEER Ove Arup & Partners
SIZE net area 13,117 square metres
TUBE Bank – Central, Northern Lines
ACCESS limited within main development; restaurant on top floor open

**James Stirling Michael Wilford & Associates**

**James Stirling Michael Wilford & Associates**

**From the City to Stansted**

**Ludgate**

Ludgate is like a baby Broadgate (see page 244), one-sixth its size and 30 per cent cheaper to build. Although from the same stable (Rosehaugh Stanhope Development), it is a more mature development. Conceived during the building mania of the mid-1980s, Ludgate has benefited from the necessity of trimming costs in the early 1990s. The buildings have become less ornate (less expensive tack) and more functional in plan and appearance, making them easier to maintain. Costs were reduced by lowering floor-to-floor heights, reducing the thickness of external walls from 300mm to 250mm, and keeping central cores as small as possible.

The 1.5-kilometre-long site straddles railway tracks going into Blackfriars. Trains were stopped for 17 days, during which time a viaduct was partly dismantled, a bridge removed, the train tracks realigned and a huge raft constructed over the tracks to form the base of the development. All the buildings rest on springs which attenuate the vibrations from the underground trains much more than the usual Neoprene pads, making the movements less jarring and the buildings effectively bouncy. The courtyard between the buildings is occupied by a painted-steel sculpture by Bruce McLean.

This project was an exercise in how to cut building costs and work with fewer staff. There was even a pilot scheme to challenge the ritual of the British workman's tea break. Bovis, the construction managers, encouraged workers to take breaks at flexible times in 'satellite' canteens on site. To avoid a complete shutdown at 9.00 when all the workers went off to the café for breakfast, it was suggested that breakfast be served on site, keeping the employees at work 20 per cent longer each day. This system has since become a common feature (even a requirement) of many large building sites, with a new generation of satellite greasy spoons now in orbit.

From the City to Stansted

**Skidmore, Owings & Merrill, Inc. 1992**

Individual buildings:
1 Ludgate Place
Skidmore, Owings & Merrill, Inc. 1992
Steel frame, panelised wall system of steel fins and aluminium spandrels.

10 Ludgate Place
Skidmore, Owings & Merrill, Inc. 1992
Steel frame with unitised system of aluminium and granite fins.

100 Ludgate Hill
Skidmore, Owings & Merrill, Inc. 1992
Reinforced-concrete structure, precast-concrete panelised system with limestone.

100 New Bridge Street
Renton Howard Wood Levin 1992
Steel frame with precast-concrete cladding.

ADDRESS Ludgate Hill, London EC4 [6B 62]
CLIENT Rosehaugh Stanhope Development plc in conjunction with British Rail Property Board
TOTAL CONTRACT VALUE £400 million
SIZE 76,250 square metres
TUBE Blackfriars – Circle, District Lines
ACCESS none

**Skidmore, Owings & Merrill, Inc. 1992**

**Skidmore, Owings & Merrill, Inc. 1992**

**Broadgate**

The City of London is the home of a strong international commercial power. During the 1980s, Thatcher's government deregulated many financial activities to open up a new age of international electronic trading. Banks and brokers merged, and started to demand a new type of office with large floorplates, floor-to-floor heights big enough to accommodate underfloor cabling, and spaces that could be flexible, could cope with 24-hour operations and would be suitable for employees working in highly stressful conditions. The demand was met between 1985 and 1991 by the addition of 4.5 million square metres of office space in central London. Broadgate provided some 334,450 square metres of this space, equal to the amount provided by five Empire State Buildings.

The site has for more than a century been a crossover point between the City and the influx of employees arriving at Liverpool Street Station. Globally, it sits between New York and Tokyo, providing a perfect base for foreign financiers.

Extensive research into client requirements revealed that North American office environments were admired: that is, the face of the buildings should be impressive and they should contain big lobbies and atriums, large open-plan office floors, and facilities that would enhance the lives of the employees – outdoor spaces, restaurants, bars and a health club. All these undertakings were achieved at Broadgate within the context of the medieval street plan and listed buildings.

The whole scheme consists of 13 buildings and three squares, built in 14 phases. The first four phases were masterminded by Arup Associates. The plan was generated from the patterns of movement of people coming to the site from Liverpool Street Station. Each phase had to be built in 12 months, taking six years in all. The secret to this speedy building system was the prefabrication of many building parts off site. Most of

**Arup Associates, Skidmore, Owings & Merrill, Inc. 1984–1991**

**Arup Associates, Skidmore, Owings & Merrill, Inc. 1984–1991**

the buildings have a steel frame with metal deck floors and external cladding to accommodate anything from an auditorium to a trading floor. Complete units, such as toilet pods, lift shafts and plant rooms, and the granite cladding with heating services incorporated, were all prefabricated and slotted into the steel frame.

More than half of the site is built on a raft which spans the railway tracks of Liverpool Street Station. Specific parts of the buildings were made by specialist fabricators under direct contract to the client in order to avoid the administrative mayhem of contractors and sub-contractors. The project involved 2200 people on site and 19,000 drawings per week, so keeping simple and direct lines of communication open was essential.

Of particular interest is Exchange House, by the Chicago firm Skidmore, Owings & Merrill, Inc. This building owes much to bridge technology since its four parabolic arches span the railway tracks. They rest on eight piers which support the entire structure. The steel-framed box that encloses the office floors hangs between the arches. This is the most expressive of all the Broadgate buildings because of the innovative technology used to create the container, articulated in the rawest of materials. The modern exterior hints at the contents of the interior, which is equipped with the most advanced information technology in Britain. The square in front gives a superb, full-length view of the inside of the vaulted train sheds at Liverpool Street Station (see page 250).

Also notable is Broadgate Square by Arup Associates, with its circular ice rink in the centre surrounded by tiered terraces, like an amphitheatre, with cascading foliage. The terraces accommodate restaurants, bars and shops behind which are the glass and granite façades of the office buildings. The square provides the desired public recreation area, but the surrounding buildings are faceless, making it seem an abrupt transition

**Arup Associates, Skidmore, Owings & Merrill, Inc. 1984–1991**

Arup Associates, Skidmore, Owings & Merrill, Inc. 1984–1991

**From the City to Stansted**

within the scheme, fully animated only at brief intervals in the day or at certain times of year. People seem to be forced to the place out of necessity rather than being drawn to it.

Helping to redeem the generally feeble architecture are the contributions by many well-known contemporary artists who were commissioned to make work especially for the site. The vast steel sheets that make up *Fulcrum* by Richard Serra rest tentatively against each other at the entrance to Broadgate Square, forming an integral part of the landscape. *Leaping Hare on Crescent and Bell* by Barry Flanagan sits in the square. The work inside 100 Liverpool Street includes a bronze horse by Flanagan, a terrazzo reception desk and mural by Bruce McLean, and prints by Patrick Caulfield.

ADDRESS Broadgate, London EC2 [5E 62]
CLIENT Rosehaugh Stanhope Development plc in conjunction with British Rail Property Board
CONSTRUCTION MANAGEMENT Bovis & Schal
SIZE 3.6 hectares
TUBE Liverpool Street – Central, Circle, Hammersmith & City, Metropolitan Lines
ACCESS public spaces are open

**Arup Associates, Skidmore, Owings & Merrill, Inc. 1984–1991**

**Arup Associates, Skidmore, Owings & Merrill, Inc. 1984–1991**

**Liverpool Street Station**

The first train arrived at Liverpool Street Station in 1875. The original L-shaped plan was determined by the two types of mainline termini the station provided. There was one long platform for the long-distance trains with its ticket offices alongside, and six short platforms for suburban trains accessible from the main concourse. The roof was built in four spans, two over the lines flanked by aisles. In 1894 eight more suburban train platforms were built to the east of the original lines, but no concourse accompanied them so they were linked by a footbridge. The roof was also extended to make a transept over the new platforms. Mass planning confusion ensued following the addition of the Underground stations.

The general plan for new engineering work on the station in the 1980s involved extending a section of the roof span on the south-west side to make a wider concourse and adding a second transept along this southern end to provide two new entrances. The shed containing the eight platforms added in 1894 has been covered by the Bishopsgate development. The north end, where open tracks once lay, is now covered by a raft structure holding Exchange House (see page 246) and a public square from which there is a superb view of the inside of the train shed and its wrought-iron roof. The contract also involved the building of a new Underground ticket hall and the relocation of the underground Post Office delivery chutes.

Inside, the cast-iron acanthus-leaf capitals supporting the roof structure have been fully restored. The design contract covered all new interventions, including the raised, covered walkway that accommodates shops and cafés and bisects the main concourse, obscuring a view of the tracks as you enter from Liverpool Street. The design of the new parts was intended to be thoroughly modern to contrast with the Victorian

**Architecture & Design Group, British Rail 1985–1991**

**Architecture & Design Group, British Rail 1985–1991**

brick shed. Admirably, there has been no attempt to mimic old styles – but the new parts are crude, adopting abstract shapes, and the structural elements are clumsy.

There are two new entrances. The one on Bishopsgate is a bizarre composition of a small square covered by a shopping-mall-type canopy flanked by two red-brick Italianate towers. These towers are repeated at the Liverpool Street entrance, but here the canopy is a piece of protruding train-shed roof, and a glass screen hangs between the towers like a portcullis ready to drop shut after the last train has departed for the night. Unfortunately, the illusion is shattered when you notice the band of sliding glass doors along the bottom that secures the station.

Each of the additions seem to have been designed in isolation, so there is a lack of overall coherence. However, the general circulation at plaform level has improved considerably and the link made between Broadgate and Bishopsgate is significant in interweaving public and private interests by way of a major railway terminus.

ADDRESS Liverpool Street/Bishopsgate, London EC2 [5E 62]
CLIENT Network South East, British Rail Board
STRUCTURAL ENGINEERS New Works Engineers, Network South East; YRM Anthony Hunt Associates; Frank Graham & Partners; De Leuw Chadwick Witham
CONTRACT VALUE £120 million
TUBE Liverpool Street – Central, Circle, Hammersmith & City, Metropolitan Lines
ACCESS open

**From the City to Stansted**

**Architecture & Design Group, British Rail 1985–1991**

**Architecture & Design Group, British Rail 1985–1991**

**Tottenham Hale Station**

Built at a time when the national railway system was threatened by privatisation, this represents the opposition to such a move by showing how the public and private sectors can work successfully together in public design (British Rail, London Underground, London Buses and the British Airport Authority all meet and co-operate at this interchange). Tottenham Hale celebrates railway architecture without nostalgia by anticipating a relaxed and more glamorous way to travel. It forms part of the journey from the high-tech Stansted Airport (see page 256) into central London, creating a stylish impression for first-time visitors.

As in many of Alsop's works, the structure and imaginative use of materials are boldly evocative of the building's function. The main external feature, a gleaming, curved, aluminium skin with portholes – containing a buffet, waiting room and lavatories – looks like the side of an aeroplane or an emerging submarine. Above this, integrated into the white steel and glass framework that spans the tracks, is a 53-metre painting by Bruce McLean on enamelled steel panels – a rare example of art which is an essential part of the architecture and not a decorative afterthought.

On a surprisingly low budget, an important and unusual architectural gesture has been made, contributing not only to a new generation of building in London, but also to the identity of the local community.

ADDRESS Ferry Lane, London N17 [4G 31]
CLIENT British Rail Network South East
ENGINEER Felix J Samuely & Partners
CONTRACT VALUE £2.3 million
TUBE Tottenham Hale – Victoria Line
BR from Liverpool Street or Stansted
ACCESS open

**From the City to Stansted**

**Alsop Lyall & Störmer 1991**

**Alsop Lyall & Störmer 1991**

**Stansted Airport**

There has been a runway at Stansted since 1942. In 1953 Stansted was singled out as London's potential third airport. Forty years and several public inquiries, reports, and committees later, the new terminal was opened by HM Queen Elizabeth II. Foster Associates became involved in the project in 1981. During the long gaps while decisions were being made in Whitehall, the time was used positively to develop a good relationship with the client.

The main design concept for the airport derived from Foster's own love of flying (he would travel to the site, stress-free, in his own helicopter) and the simplicity of early airport terminals. The open fields of Stansted invited a low, single-storey building with a roadside entrance and car park on one side and the runway and aeroplane satellites on the other.

Travellers by rail arrive underneath the building and are transported via an escalator or lifts directly into the main concourse. Check-ins, shops, security areas and departure lounge are arranged in a linear fashion to avoid excessive signage and disorientation, with views out to the runway throughout. A monorail shuttle whisks passengers to the adjacent satellite for boarding. This ease of passage was informed by many hours spent in airports while the architects flew back and forth from Hong Kong during the construction of the Hongkong & Shanghai Bank.

The vast open space of the main building is clearly articulated by the spectacular roof structure that floats more than 15 metres above our heads. A quilt of square domes is supported by a grid of 36 service trees. The white roof membrane (perforated steel trays and insulated Sarnafil PVC) filters light down on to the grey terrazzo floor and reflects light from inside. The domes also act as smoke reservoirs with extractor fans built into the top of each tree. Another significant achievement in the design of the roof is the syphonic draining system which allows drainpipes to

**Foster Associates 1985–1991**

**Foster Associates 1985–1991**

be laid horizontally. All air-conditioning, information and lighting services are contained in the roof support/service pods, leaving the concourse space completely free of pipes and ducts. Travellers and airport staff can see the sky, the aeroplanes and the fields through the glazed perimeter walls all around. Remarkably, a highly technical and structurally sophisticated enclosure exudes the qualities of a natural environment.

Interior detailing was never treated as a separate issue by the architects. Everything from carpets and seating to check-in desks has been given obsessive consideration and each item has been custom-made for this particular terminal. Even the white, fire-proof retail 'cabins' have been rigorously designed so that they disguise loud shop logos and unsightly trad brass fittings. Check-in desks are made from a kit of stainless-steel and linoleum-covered plywood parts that can be rearranged easily as more airlines move to Stansted.

It is anticipated that 8 million passengers a year will pass through the terminal by the end of this century, and there will be space to accommodate 15 million in the future. I hope that the surrounding infrastructure, the road and rail links, provide the necessary back-up.

ADDRESS Stansted, Essex
CLIENT British Airport Authority/Stansted Airport Limited
STRUCTURAL ENGINEER Ove Arup & Partners
CONTRACT VALUE £400 million
SIZE main terminal is 39,000 square metres
BR Stansted is approximately 40 minutes from Liverpool Street or Tottenham Hale
ROAD just off M11
ACCESS open

**Foster Associates 1985–1991**

**Foster Associates 1985–1991**

# Hackney to Stratford

# Cullinan/Harbour Houses

1998 saw the tenth anniversary of the purchase of this site by two young architects who were designing office blocks in conventional practices at the time (hence their familiarity with concrete for the primary structure). Ivan Harbour is now an associate at the Richard Rogers Partnership; Dominic Cullinan was working in Ian Ritchie's office but has since set up his own practice. Ten years later the building is by no means finished.

From the outset the intention was to build a home for each partner and to build it themselves as cashflow permitted. The initial plan envisaged a house at the front of the site and one at the rear backing on to a parking lot, but the buildings would have been too close for facing properties. Today two four-storey homes sit side by side facing the street, with a garden at the rear and a glorified garden shed, backing on to the parking lot, which has functioned as everything from home to Cullinan and family to kitchen for Harbour and family while they install a permanent kitchen facility in their house.

The two houses grow outwards from a stairwell that provides a shared structural core for the whole building. This core is leaf-shaped in plan and takes the double helix of a DNA strand as its form, so the space left behind by one spiral is occupied by another winding in the opposite direction. For a grand comparison, the stair tower at the Chateau de Blois (1508), attributed to Leonardo da Vinci, performs a similar function. A more utilitarian example is the fire-escape stairs inserted in many US office blocks. The double strand uses space efficiently while maintaining separate means of access.

The plan of each house is long and narrow and they are naturally lit through full-height glazing on the front and rear elevations. The narrow plan is compensated by generous floor-to-ceiling heights, with the first floor cut away at the rear to create a double-height space on the ground

**Dominic Cullinan and Ivan Harbour 1988–**

**Dominic Cullinan and Ivan Harbour 1988–**

floor. The stairs emerge at the top of each house into a crow's-nest room then continue on to a roof terrace, creating a lightwell over the stair. Windows on the front elevation are lined in an opaque corrugated plastic that both insulates and obscures direct views into the houses.

Harbour describes the project as 'evolutionary' rather than 'revolutionary', and the building has come about by purely organic means (it took six months to make the formwork for each section of the stair core and one hour to pour it, hence each pour was a different experience). The building team comprised juniors at Ove Arup & Partners who tried out their engineering skills (there is more concrete below ground than above), several generations of students from the Architectural Association and willing family members. The same limited budget encouraged the acquisition of a magpie's nest of left-over materials collected from building merchants and sites.

The Hackney Society wants to list the houses as one of its significant buildings of the twentieth century – perhaps the first time an unfinished building has been deemed worthy of such reverence. An inspiration to any would-be self-builder.

ADDRESS 1 Trumans Road, London N16 [5F 47]
STRUCTURAL ENGINEER ongoing advice from participating employees of Ove Arup & Partners
SIZE 260-square-metre site
NORTH LONDON LINE Dalston Kingsland
ACCESS contact Dominic Cullinan Architecture on 0171–923 7100

**Dominic Cullinan and Ivan Harbour 1988–**

**Dominic Cullinan and Ivan Harbour 1988–**

# Twentieth-Century Wing

### Geffrye Museum

The Geffrye Museum – formerly the almshouses of the Worshipful Company of Ironmongers (built 1715) and now Grade-1 listed – specialises in the furniture and domestic interiors of the urban middle classes, with period rooms laid out in sequence from 1600 to 1900. In 1990 an additional wing was planned to bring the displays up to the present day.

One of the first and largest buildings to be awarded funds from the lottery, the new wing houses the twentieth-century rooms, a new restaurant and shop, a gallery space for temporary displays, a design centre for work by local craftsmen, a store for items not on display, and two education studios. The design process was closely monitored by English Heritage and the Hackney Society, both of whom were keen to see the new wing as a building in its own right without attempting to ape the Queen Anne style of the almshouses. The main concerns were the way the old and new would meet and that any new structure would not impose on the symmetry of the existing buildings.

On entering the main gates of the museum there is no evidence of the new extension. The land falling away at the south-eastern corner behind the main buildings accommodates a two-storey construction by sinking the lower floor into the ground. The new site protrudes into the urban landscape of a disused railway line, a late 1980s office development and the backs of houses, and it was the challenge of pulling together these incongruous parts to create some kind of urban unity that excited the architects and resulted in this long, bendy, brick and timber-raftered shed with a slate roof. The horseshoe-shaped plan enables the continuation of the linear progression of displays while fitting into a smaller site.

The glass-wrapped transitional space between the eighteenth-century right-angled walls of the former almshouses and Branson Coates' obliquely angled spaces forms a semi-outdoor room for a restaurant and

**Branson Coates Architecture 1998**

**Branson Coates Architecture 1998**

shop. Key elements are picked out and expressed as sculptural gestures to re-emphasise the distinction between old and new and to clarify a logical means of circulation within the new building: a suspended ceiling made on a diagrid pattern floats through the common areas, helping to direct visitors through the space. The gently contoured surface draws the eye down the middle of the plan to the permanent displays around the windowless curved back of the building. The ceiling is suspended in such a way as to provide clerestory lighting to the central space, above a cast-concrete spiral stair with a scaly glass balustrade and copper rainwater pipes forming the central pillar which leads to the ancillary facilities at semi-basement level. A sloped ha-ha dug around the base of the building allows daylight to penetrate the lower level.

The use of traditional materials and the modelling of the interior spaces reflect the scale and intimacy of the eighteenth-century buildings while twisting their original meaning: exterior brick walls are built on sloping courses in a continuous curve creating the illusory effect of a mobius strip, though all walls are built with lime mortar and without expansion joints in the traditional way. The new wing is absolutely the 'sympathetic partner with a spirit of its own' that Nigel Coates first envisaged.

ADDRESS Kingsland Road, London E2 [2E 62]
STRUCTURAL ENGINEER Alan Baxter Associates
CONTRACT VALUE £5.3 million
SIZE 1900 square metres
TUBE Liverpool Street – Central, Circle, Hammersmith & City,
Metropolitan Lines; Old Street – Northern Line
ACCESS open Tuesday to Saturday 10.00–17.00; Sunday 14.00–17.00

**Branson Coates Architecture 1998**

**Branson Coates Architecture 1998**

# Hackney Community College

This is one of the largest new further-education campuses in the UK, running vocational training courses, adult- and community-education classes and a Sixth Form Centre. These courses were formerly provided through 13 college centres and more than 80 outreach venues throughout the borough. The new Shoreditch Campus has become one of two principal sites (the other is at Brooke House), housing two-thirds of the college (14,000 full- and part-time students), a public library and a one-stop shop for the council. The other venues are being sold and the proceeds put back into the new campuses. The college has grown by 25 per cent over the last four years and has established strong links with local employers and the community sector.

Phase 1 of the development was completed in 1997. Phase 3 (the Art, Design and Media Centre) is due for completion towards the end of 1998. Phase 2 (the Sports Centre) has not broken ground yet. Phases 2 and 3 spread eastwards from the main campus to meet Kingsland Road.

The key elements of the design were developed by Sir Colin Stansfield-Smith of Hampshire County Architects, the godfather of that county's outstanding primary-school programme. The central theme of many of the Hampshire schools was the creation of a micro-habitat that centres on a communal space (a street or square) to which other areas have direct access. The Shoreditch Campus is planned around such a defensible space. Here the plan focuses on two large courtyards, one of which is bisected by two three-storey Edwardian school buildings refurbished by Hawkins Brown.

The design concept of standardised three-storey blocks linked by vertical service cores is well suited to phased construction and flexibility. The blocks have concrete frames clad in buff brickwork and high-performance aluminium-framed glazing, with pitched roofs made of glue-

**Hampshire County Architects/Percy Ogden Architects 1997**

**Hampshire County Architects/Percy Ogden Architects 1997**

laminated timber beams and insulated metal cladding. Ventilation is on the whole by natural means via openable windows and rooflights.

In order that the primary north (Falkirk Street) and west (Hoxton Street) boundary walls did not read as battlements from the outside, a series of artist-designed gates and screens has been incorporated into the brickwork to allow views into the campus and maintain a sense of scale with the surrounding streets. The Edwardian school buildings have been retained to provide general teaching, social and crèche facilities and a context that enriches the much larger areas of new building. Mature plane trees have also been retained to enhance the external areas.

The main entrance on Falkirk Street is at the corner of the north courtyard: a large, hard-landscaped area surrounded on three sides by three-storey blocks that house the new library, teaching areas and administration facilities. The Learning Resource Centre is in the middle of the courtyard at semi-basement level and connects underground to the library. The centre is approached via a sunken amphitheatre on one side and is flanked on the other by a water feature bordered by a 2-metre-long blue wall designed by sculptor Susanna Heron (other artworks include the benches around the amphitheatre by Bettina Furnee, a ceramic fountain by Lotte Glob, gates by Matthew Fedden and stone seats in the south courtyard by Pat Kaufman). Two shallow, glazed protrusions emerging from the landscaped roof of the centre allow natural light into the subterranean room. The smaller south courtyard is soft-landscaped and is dominated by the two Edwardian buildings.

The main circulation routes are a key feature of the internal courtyards. The routes are defined by perimeter colonnades formed from a skeletal hardwood structure that reaches to the full height of the buildings. The structure also accommodates high-level sun louvres and lower-level

**Hampshire County Architects/Percy Ogden Architects 1997**

**Hampshire County Architects/Percy Ogden Architects 1997**

membrane canopies to provide shelter from the rain.

Much of the success of the project can be attributed to the decisions of the college directors to involve local residents from the outset and to appoint their own project managers from within the college to oversee the works and make sure the college's needs were met. Hackney has some of the highest rates of poverty and poor housing in Britain, the highest rate of unemployment of any London borough, and 33.6 per cent of its population is made up of minority ethnic groups, the majority of whom do not speak English as their first language. If any London neighbourhood needs a facility of this quality it is this one – and it should serve as a solid model for councils to adopt. Better still, make it a standard national requirement.

ADDRESS Shoreditch Campus, Falkirk Street, London N1 [2E 62]
CLIENTS Hackney Community College/Shoreditch Project Team on behalf of principal funders: Further Education Funding Council, Dalston City Partnership, European Regional Development Fund, Hackney Community College, London Borough of Hackney, Sports Council Lottery
STRUCTURAL ENGINEER Buro Happold (phase 1); Whitby & Bird (phases 2 and 3)
CONTRACT VALUE approximately £40 million
SIZE 27,000 square-metre site; phase 1: 19,600 square metres of new buildings
TUBE Old Street – Northern Line
ACCESS by appointment only – enquiries to Jacqui Hurst on 0171 613 9125/9034

**Hampshire County Architects/Percy Ogden Architects 1997**

**Hampshire County Architects/Percy Ogden Architects 1997**

**Rushton Street Medical Centre**

The medical centre has emerged recently as a new building type in our architectural vocabulary. It can be traced back to the Tomlinson Report in the mid 1980s and a subsequent government initiative called 'Making London Better' which identified that the standards of local health services in London needed to be raised, including the condition of the buildings that housed GPs' practices. In 1993 the London Implementation Group set up publicly funded London Initiative Zones where the Family Health Services Authority (FHSA) and local health authorities were to acquire, manage and develop premises. The FHSA then took on the role of promoter and co-ordinator of such projects.

South Hoxton is an area where none of the existing GPs' practices was suitable for development. So the practices merged and worked closely with the architects to develop a brief for a new building that would provide primary healthcare services for the area, be easily recognisable to the community as a building for health, and act as a catalyst for development.

The three-storey frontage faces north across Shoreditch Park. The linear plan is based around a top-lit central street on the ground floor (similar to the influential plans for schools laid out by Hampshire County Architects – see page 270) subdivided to accommodate the individual practices but with the potential to be opened up to respond to future changes in the occupants' requirements. The street serves as a central communication zone and is the main waiting area, with offices, treatment and consulting rooms to either side. The main circulation stair is at the eastern end of the building, set back from the main façade. A section of the ground floor had to be given over to car parking so the largest of the four practices moved up to the first floor. A third storey (on the north-facing side only) is for office use and a caretaker's flat. The roof rises in

**Penoyre & Prasad Architects 1997**

**Penoyre & Prasad Architects 1997**

a wave-like form to create a double-height space over the corner of a multi-purpose room at this level which is for community classes.

The cutting back of the ground floor on the front elevation has prompted a series of overhangs from the upper floors which shelter the surgery entrances (each marked by a slender column). The rippling wall of timber fins and glass on the first floor is a response to the way that the consulting rooms inside are used – hand-washing basins are set into the curved bays to create a degree of privacy between doctor and patient and neighbouring consulting rooms. The progression from brick base to timber and rendered walls echoes the London vernacular, while the plans, animated elevations and strong use of colour reflect more modern influences (for instance, Lubetkin and Tecton's Finsbury Health Centre, 1938, in Pine Street, EC1).

See also the Melbourne Grove Medical Practice, East Dulwich by Wharmby Kozdon Architects; the Portobello Health Centre, West London by Pentarch Architects; Elm Trees Surgery, Greenford, West London by Sandhu Architects; and the Island Health Medical Centre, Isle of Dogs by John Duane Architects.

ADDRESS 6–12 Rushton Street, London N1 [2D 62]
CLIENT East London and City Health Authority/Imperial Square Developments
STRUCTURAL ENGINEER Whitby & Bird
CONTRACT VALUE £1.3 million
SIZE 1400 square metres
TUBE Old Street – Northern Line
ACCESS limited

**Penoyre & Prasad Architects 1997**

**Penoyre & Prasad Architects 1997**

# Three Mills Bridge and Three Mills Island Landscaping

Three Mills Island sits in the middle of Mill Meads, a large area of heavy- and light-industrial buildings. The island (surrounded by the narrow waterways of Bow Creek) is home to a sports centre and a distillery.

A new bridge was required to allow industrial traffic on to the island and a square and a new entrance to the sports ground were also incorporated into the scheme. The engineering of the heavy-duty bridge, spanning 30 metres, is consistent with the construction techniques of the eighteenth-century mill buildings on its south side: the principal spans are formed of welded-plate girders with secondary steels spanning transversely between them. The road surface is an open steel mesh with a separate pedestrian deck cantilevered from below the south girder.

The south girder is extended in length and animated by an artwork (by Peter Fink) of punctured holes and metal studs and sleeves. A kite shape marked with diverging lines of granite defines the square. The sports ground gate is flanked by two walls: the 'sign wall' incorporates advertisements and information while the other side is made up of various gates including an anti-motorcycle gate, a disabled radar gate, a children's gate and a pets' gate. The whole is a successful meshing of the disciplines of architecture, engineering, landscaping and art.

ADDRESS Three Mill Lane, London E3 [3E 64]
CLIENT London Industrial (Three Mills Bridge), Lea Valley Regional Park Authority (landscape works) supported by the Stratford Development Partnership
STRUCTURAL ENGINEER Marks Healey Brothwell
TUBE Bromley-by-Bow – District Line
ACCESS open

**Clash Associates 1997**

**Clash Associates 1997**

# Abbey Mills Pumping Station

The above-ground enclosure used less than 7 per cent of the overall budget. Much of the major engineering project lies underground inside a reinforced-concrete substructure incorporating new low-level culverts which pump sewage to be discharged at a higher level. Pumping equipment is at ground-floor level with a central spine at first-floor level for the generators and switchgear. Air intakes and extracts protrude from this central spine and through the roof on either side.

The extruded section is shaped by the substructure and provides a smooth bubble of gleaming metal cladding around the superstructure. Steel portal frames form side aisles which support catwalks for equipment maintenance. The central spine is made up of similar portal frames with bow-string roof beams spanning between inner and outer portals.

The deep pitch of the roof allows the building to lie low in a landscape that is to be converted into meadowland. The pumping station's precursor (1865–68) stands adjacent to the site (retained for storm pumping) – an outstanding example of Victorian engineering by Joseph Bazalgette that uses Moorish, Byzantine and Gothic features to disguise its identity. Allies & Morrison allude to these references in the shape of their roof, but they express the function of the building through a scale and materials.

ADDRESS Abbey Lane, London E15 [2F 65]
STRUCTURAL ENGINEER Ove Arup & Partners (superstructure)/Trafalgar House Technology (substructure)
CONTRACT VALUE £2 million (enclosure)/£30 million whole project
TUBE Bromley-by-Bow – District Line
ACCESS none

**Allies & Morrison 1997**

**Allies & Morrison 1997**

# Playground Canopy

**St Anne's Infant School**

This project was initiated by the BBC as part of a television series called *Public Property*. Architects and designers were invited to make new interventions in neglected public areas. The tensile-membrane structure rises in two peaks supported by telegraph poles inside and capped with metal cones outside, then swoops down to a low, curved arch to form the mouth of the canopy. The landscaped floor plan beneath is built up to make an auditorium shape from stepped levels of hard-core covered in a spongey finish and edged in telegraph poles.

The outdoor classroom breaks new ground in the world of tensile-membrane structures in several ways. In particular, the tension rods have been lifted up to above ground level so that children do not trip on them; gravel around the bases of the posts discourages running. The caps act as ventilators at the top of the canopy, and it is the first time that coloured shapes have been cut into tensional fabric. Colours are used to highlight tension points and blue ridges act as gutters.

The canopy is a joyful and innovative creation which sits menacingly beside uninspiring classroom huts. It was the first time this particular firm of architects had designed a tensile-membrane structure, so the project was an adventure for everyone.

ADDRESS Hunton Street, London E1 [5G 63]
CLIENT St Anne's School
STRUCTURAL ENGINEER YRM Anthony Hunt Associates: Hanif Kara
TUBE Whitechapel – District, Hammersmith & City Lines
BUS 25, 253 to Whitechapel
ACCESS view from the street or inside by prior appointment only

**McCormac Jamieson Prichard 1994**

**McCormac Jamieson Prichard 1994**

# Swanlea Secondary School

This is the first new secondary school to be built in London in the last ten years. It is designed to accommodate 1050 pupils, with meeting rooms for use outside school hours. More significantly, the layout and size of the classrooms and communication between them have been informed by the demands of the National Curriculum (set out by the Conservative government in 1990), making it the first school of its kind. The scheme has created a new focus and social centre for a community which is culturally rich but economically run-down.

The plan focuses on a central covered street or mall, lined by London-stock brick buildings which in turn surround a series of courtyards and gardens on the south side of the mall and a car park on the north side. The dramatic sweep of the glass mall roof greets you on Brady Street and draws you into the heart of the scheme: an avenue flanked by curved, tapered columns bowing like trees in the wind, restrained by clusters of diagonal struts which support the glazing. The method of passive solar-energy recovery means that during winter the mall acts as a heat source for the whole scheme. The glazed roof is made up of Okasolar Glass panels (a specialised glass made up of prismatic strips that reflect the high summer sun and let in low winter sun), which provide a much cheaper and more efficient alternative to blinds. During the summer the mall is ventilated at a high level, creating cross-ventilation vertically through the space without the expense and dubious environmental impact of air-conditioning. Classrooms have shop windows fronting the mall so that work can be presented to the school community and to make maximum use of natural light, heat and ventilation. This seems to be a tremendous success, though many of the classrooms may not prove to be adaptable enough given the constant changes in curriculum requirements.

The gardens are outdoor classrooms: one is an ecological garden,

**Percy Thomas Partnership/Hampshire County Architects 1991–1993**

**Percy Thomas Partnership/Hampshire County Architects 1991–1993**

another an exhibition courtyard. Eerily marking the south-west corner of the site is the caretaker's house, which is a stop-off point on the Jack the Ripper bus tour, for this site was where the monster gruesomely finished off many of his victims.

The architects have responded to this semi-wasteland by making a positive statement which follows through from the imaginative overall plan as far as possible into the details, within a very tight budget.

ADDRESS Brady Street, London E1 [4H 63]
CLIENT London Borough of Tower Hamlets Education Department
STRUCTURAL ENGINEER YRM Anthony Hunt Associates
CONTRACT VALUE £9.2 million
SIZE 10,500 square metres
TUBE Whitechapel – District, Hammersmith & City Lines
BUS 25, 253 to Whitechapel
ACCESS limited

**Percy Thomas Partnership/Hampshire County Architects 1991–1993**

**Stratford Market Depot**

Having failed to win the bid for the Jubilee Line Extension station at London Bridge, the practice did well to win its first major commission here at Stratford instead. An outline scheme, fee bid and management proposal for a train shed (for the inspection and maintenance of 11 trains), control building (to survey a secure area for 33 trains adjacent to the main shed), workshops and stores, offices and amenities and a traction substation were compiled in two weeks, with the finished building remaining remarkably true to the early plans.

The site was determined by the archeological remains of a medieval abbey found to its east and the layout of the existing tracks. Safety requires that tracks straighten out before entering a building, thus determining the 30-degree cut-off angle of the front entrance and the consequent parallelogram plan. All administrative and amenities buildings are lined up regimentally in grey uniforms along the west side of the main shed, each unit designed to suit its function while using common construction details.

The train-shed roof is a 100-metre-long, gently curving span with clear headroom of 8 metres above the tracks. The roof structure is a space frame formed on a diagrid rather than on a conventional orthogonal grid because of the angles produced by the parallelogram plan. Two rows of columns form divisions between the three categories of internal operations in the building, thus enabling the overall roof span to be reduced. Each concrete-filled steel column extends into three branched arms to carry the load and meet the space frame at regular intervals. The v-shaped pattern of the columns on the long elevations provides lateral stability while the tracery created by the columns and space frame, painted white and pale green respectively, enhances the lightness of the vast structure. Daylight is admitted from all sides of the building: through the roof (stri-

**Chris Wilkinson Architects 1997**

**Chris Wilkinson Architects 1997**

ated with openable rooflights), the south wall (clad in translucent fibre-glass), clerestory glazing in the side walls, and the north wall, which is made of a special suspended-glass system purpose-designed in conjunction with Pilkington.

One of the client's conditions was that the architect and structural engineer should have equal rights as lead consultants, to build a co-operative relationship from the outset. The building demonstrates the effectiveness of this way of working, with neither party attempting to gain ground over the other by obscuring aspects of the design process or adding unnecessary elements for effect. As with all good industrial buildings, the Stratford Market Depot and its ancillary structures are unhampered by the daunting lack of context and stand out as pure expressions of function, structure and materials.

ADDRESS Angel Lane, London E15 [6F 49]
CLIENT London Underground
STRUCTURAL ENGINEER Hyder Consulting
CONTRACT VALUE approximately £18 million
SIZE 11-hectare site (main shed 19,000 square metres)
TUBE Stratford – Central Line
ACCESS very limited

**Chris Wilkinson Architects 1997**

**Chris Wilkinson Architects 1997**

# Stratford Bus Station

Like a tent in the desert, the bus-station canopy is a welcome retreat from the jammed one-way system that strangles a desolate suburban borough centre. It is the first in a series of new transport buildings planned for East London alongside the extension of the Jubilee Line (see page 326) and additions to the Docklands Light Railway (see page 316). The roof canopy rises gracefully above the bedlam. It is made up of tensile-fabric inverted umbrellas supported by a forest of steel columns set out on a grid to define the main waiting area. Each column contains channels for roof drainage and cable conduit for lighting. The inverted-canopy form allows double-decker buses to draw up to the stop beneath the shelter. Concourse services are encased in building blocks around the perimeter of the sheltered area and clad in graffiti-proof glass panels.

Despite clear sightlines throughout the concourse, the absence of blind corners and enclosed spaces and the generous glazed screens shielding the waiting rooms, the structure is still draped in an assortment of security paraphernalia such as video monitors and loudspeakers.

ADDRESS Great Eastern Road, London E15 [7F 49]
CLIENT London Transport Buses
IN-HOUSE ARCHITECT Soji Abass
STRUCTURAL ENGINEER Anthony Hunt Associates
CONTRACT VALUE £2 million
DOCKLANDS LIGHT RAILWAY Stratford
TUBE Stratford – Central Line
ACCESS open

**London Bus Transport Passenger Infrastructure 1994**

Hackney to Stratford

**Hackney to Stratford**

**London Bus Transport Passenger Infrastructure 1994**

# Docklands

# Storm-Water Pumping Station

The building houses a control and supply-maintenance room for the electric pumps which are in chambers under the floor. When storm water flows from the Isle of Dogs into the underfloor chamber it is raised automatically into a concrete surge tank high above ground level and then forced by gravity into the Thames. The building is terrorist-proof and its concrete substructure is able to withstand an explosion. These factors explain why it is so massive in scale. Once you get over the sheer size and realise that the 3-metre-diameter propeller does actually rotate at 16 rpm to evacuate gases that may build up inside, and appreciate the detailing that shows no signs of ageing (after all it was built to last 100 years), you realise you are looking at a windowless shed. It is also a monument, 'a temple for summer storms'.

Colours and materials link directly with the iconography: slate-blue bricks signify the river which flows through the two vast trees (columns) on the front and back façades, and red and yellow stripes signify the mountainside from which the water flows. The columns are not supporting the lightweight pediment but are disguising steps and ducts. Each element of the building has been embellished in a manner which portrays Outram's own imagination and fascination with assembling and exaggerating historical symbols.

ADDRESS Stewart Street, Isle of Dogs, London E1 [2E 80]
CLIENT London Docklands Development Corporation/Thames Water
STRUCTURAL ENGINEER Sir William Halcrow & Partners
CONTRACT VALUE £3.5 million
SIZE approximately 670 square metres
DOCKLANDS LIGHT RAILWAY South Quay
ACCESS none

**John Outram 1988**

Docklands

**John Outram 1988**

# Jack Dash House
## Isle of Dogs Neighbourhood Centre

Jack Dash House is the result of a collaboration between a developer, a borough council and a firm of architects who are more widely known for their refurbishment of West End clubs. It is unusual because it is a strong public building in an area which is a dishevelled monument to Thatcherite free-market economics. The building is named after the dockers' leader who died in 1989 but who had campaigned vigorously in his later life against the encroaching Canary Wharf development.

The plan is made up of three sides around a courtyard. The arterial west wing accommodates offices (highly insulated and naturally ventilated), the north wing contains a crèche which doubles as a theatre space and the south side forms the main entrance and link to the round tower which contains the Council Chamber and a gallery space below.

The costs of the building were kept very low by using the design-and-build method of construction where the architects design the building but the contractor is responsible for all construction. This means that detailing is often compromised. Despite this, the building stands out and represents a local council that has the flare to provide an imaginative working environment and a useful public space for the community.

ADDRESS Marsh Wall, London E14 [1C 80]
CLIENT London Docklands Development Corporation (for the London Borough of Tower Hamlets)
STRUCTURAL ENGINEER Price & Myers
CONTRACT VALUE £4.5 million
SIZE 4460 square metres
DOCKLANDS LIGHT RAILWAY South Quay
ACCESS open

Docklands

**Chassay Architects 1990**

**Chassay Architects 1990**

**Control Centre and Lifting Bridges**

In the shadow of the monstrous Canary Wharf development, the gleaming Control Centre has invented an unselfconscious architecture all of its own. Starting with the design intention of revealing all the bridges' working parts, the architects have ingeniously created a separate building to house the hydraulic plant required to operate the counterweight system of the lifting bridges.

The simple steel-frame and steel-panel construction (welded on site) has been stretched and details exaggerated to create a bold, sculptural form. Each feature – gutter, air vents, staircase and control cabin – is an integral part of the structure, not a decorative afterthought. The great A-frames, pivots and hydraulic rams are now in full view, as are the mooring platform, fishing platform and public staircase – all dramatic silver elements set against the primary white structure of the bridges.

Many of these bascule bridges can be found in and around Chicago. This one, however, remains symbolic rather than practical as at present ocean liners do not navigate these docks.

ADDRESS Canary Wharf, Eastern Access, London E14 [80 E1]
CLIENT London Docklands Development Corporation
ENGINEER Mott MacDonald Civil Limited
COST £4 million
DOCKLANDS LIGHT RAILWAY Canary Wharf
ACCESS none

Docklands

**Alsop Lyall & Störmer 1990**

**Alsop Lyall & Störmer 1990**

**Cascades**

Twenty storeys high, with water on two sides, Cascades holds its head up defiantly in the middle of low-lying Docklands. From a distance the block seems to be a formidable solid lump with an unusual leaning profile, but close up it becomes multi-faceted, made up of layers of windows, balconies, turrets and portholes. The texture of the façades is a result of the plan. A spinal corridor runs through the centre, to either side of which are one-, two- and three-bedroom flats set at angles to capture interesting views and light. The flats have deep, open plans with small cabin bedrooms tucked at the back (nearest the corridor). The sloping side is the fire-escape stair accommodated in a long, shed-shaped enclosure (like a greenhouse) with roof terraces at each side. The view is spectacular. Facilities include a swimming pool (at the bottom of the slope), gymnasium, conference room and some shops.

Cascades has been described as 'a castle for men and women of the right stuff', the types who people Tom Wolfe's novel *Bonfire of the Vanities*. The block is a symbol of the 1980s boom in finance and property, when young professionals came to settle here attracted by the proximity of the City and what seemed a good investment given Canary Wharf rising nearby. But now many residents have become disillusioned, stranded in a location that still lacks such basic amenities as a decent transport system.

ADDRESS West Ferry Road, London E14 [1C 80]
CLIENT Kentish Homes
CONTRACT VALUE £18.8 million
SIZE 164 flats
DOCKLANDS LIGHT RAILWAY South Quay
ACCESS none

**CZWG Architects 1986–1988**

Docklands

**CZWG Architects 1986–1988**

# Canary Wharf

The late Francis Tibbalds, writing in *The Architects' Journal* (7 November 1990), nicely summed up Europe's largest single development:

> If you want to see what, left to its own devices, the private sector produces, one need look no further than the Isle of Dogs in London's Docklands. The British Government's flagship of 'enterprise culture development' and the urban design challenge of the century adds up to little more than market-led, opportunistic chaos – an architectural circus – with a sprinkling of Post-Modern gimmicks, frenzied construction of the megalumps of Canary Wharf and a fairground train to get you there. It is a disappointment to those who live and work there. Sadly, there was a necessary intermediate step between balance sheet and building that got missed in the rush. It is called urban design.

Canary Wharf, excavated in the 1800s, is part of the Isle of Dogs. The warehouses then were the largest in Europe, some up to 1000 metres long. The port was abandoned at the beginning of the 1980s. At the same time, the Thatcher government set up the Urban Development Corporation to regenerate inner cities and to bring together the interests of business and property developers. The Isle of Dogs was declared an 'Enterprise Zone', to be monitored by the London Docklands Development Corporation. Emphasis shifted from creating places that would be accessible to and would serve the public to market-led priorities: buildings for particular types of people, and especially for international business.

Canary Wharf was conceived as Britain's new financial centre and one of the three major financial centres of the world, alongside New York and Tokyo. It was believed that the City's older buildings would not be able to cope with the demands of computerisation and a growing business

**Docklands**

**Skidmore, Owings & Merrill, Inc. (masterplanners) 1988–1991**

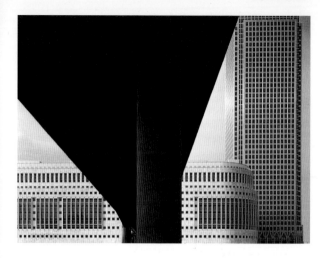

**Skidmore, Owings & Merrill, Inc. (masterplanners) 1988–1991**

population. The development initially suffered from poor transport links, but with the completion of the Limehouse Link Tunnel there is now a direct route by car from the City following the line of the river, while with the arrival of its own station on the Jubilee Line Extension (designed by Sir Norman Foster & Partnerss, see page 332) Canary Wharf could at last occupy its intended strategic position in the east of London.

The site is long and thin with buildings of about 14 storeys around a central square. The plan claims to incorporate the patterns of London's Regency squares but there is little in either its scale or proportion to substantiate this. The buildings are more 1930s Chicago in scale (and most of the architects involved in the project are American firms).

The landmark is obviously the tower by Cesar Pelli. He describes it as: 'a square prism with pyramidal top in the traditional form of the obelisk, which is the most archetypal way of creating a vertical architectural sign ... this is the essence of the skyscraper.' It is the first skyscraper to be clad in stainless steel. Pelli used the material to symbolise the high-tech nature of the activities inside and to reflect what light there is falling on the building. He would have preferred the tower to be taller and more slender, but the LDDC had already laid down rigid sizes for floor plans and heights. Five floors were consequently sliced off the top in order not to obstruct the nearby flight path.

The architects employed on Canary Wharf were really required to design façades for speculative office blocks, the size and shape of which had been predetermined, so the challenge for each one was to produce a sufficiently bland frontage to suit any occupant. The elevations and the interiors have separate logics. The result is variations on a theme: an international style of classical colonnades, single windows rather than bands of glass, and stripes of stone cladding.

**Docklands**

### Skidmore, Owings & Merrill, Inc. (masterplanners) 1988–1991

**Skidmore, Owings & Merrill, Inc. (masterplanners) 1988–1991**

It remains to be seen whether Canary Wharf will become a twenty-first-century metropolis – certainly there have been no holds barred as far as further development in the immediate area is concerned. Perhaps the arrival of the Jubilee Line will help to draw more people to the site, but in the meantime it still stands as a symbol of 1980s' smash-and-grab culture.

Buildings and architects include:

1 Cabot Square – Pei, Cobb, Freed & Partners
10 Cabot Square – Skidmore, Owings & Merrill, Inc.
20 Cabot Square – Kohn Pederson Fox
25 Cabot Square – Skidmore, Owings & Merrill, Inc.
25 The North Colonnade – Troughton McAslan
30 The South Colonnade – Kohn Pederson Fox
1 Canada Square/Cabot Place/Docklands Light Railway Station – Cesar Pelli & Associates

ADDRESS Isle of Dogs, London E14 [D1 80]
DEVELOPER Olympia & York Canary Wharf Limited
CONTRACT VALUE approximately £750 million
SIZE 28.3 hectares
DOCKLANDS LIGHT RAILWAY Canary Wharf
BUS D5, P14 to Canary Wharf
ACCESS public spaces open

**Skidmore, Owings & Merrill, Inc. (masterplanners) 1988–1991**

**Skidmore, Owings & Merrill, Inc. (masterplanners) 1988–1991**

**Thames Barrier**

The Visitors' Centre (for a nominal charge of £2.25, and the handbook at £2.95) will provide you with detailed information about the construction and workings of the Thames Barrier in a typically early 1980s multi-media way, set to an equally suspect rock-opera soundtrack to heighten your experience of this genuinely remarkable engineering feat. The best bit is a model of the barrier that rotates to demonstrate its actions at an intelligible scale.

The need for such a barrier arose from two main factors: the rise in the high-water level at London Bridge by about 750mm a century due to the melting of the polar ice caps; and the action of surge tides which originate as zones of atmospheric pressure off the coast of Canada. Where the warm Gulf Stream meets the cold Labrador Current the sea is raised approximately 300mm. This hump of water moves across the Atlantic and occasionally northerly winds force it down the North Sea, sending millions of tonnes of extra water up the Thames.

Between 1953 and 1970 many schemes were proposed for different types and locations of barrages, guillotine gates and retractable bridges. One and a quarter million people spread over 116 square kilometres were at risk, so in 1970 the Greater London Council was given responsibility for the whole flood-prevention scheme. The width of the river is divided by piers to form six openings for shipping and four subsidiary non-navigational openings. Reinforced-concrete piers founded on coffer dams (watertight boxes of interlocking steel plates) support a rotating circular arm to which are fixed the silver, moon-shaped gates. The seating for the gates is provided by concrete sills, containing service ducts, which were cast, then sunk to the level of the chalk riverbed. The largest sill measures 60 x 27 x 8.5 metres and weighs 10,000 tonnes.

The gates themselves – four of 1500 tonnes and two of 750 tonnes –

**Docklands**

**GLC Department of Architecture 1984**

**GLC Department of Architecture 1984**

were manufactured at Darlington. These colossal elements had to be manoeuvred to within a maximum tolerance of 10mm, fixed by divers working in zero visibility. The upturned hull-shaped roofs not only act as the symbolic feature of the barrier above water level but also protect the operating machinery – reversible hydaulic rams that rotate the gates into any one of four positions. The roofs have timber shells covered with maintenance-free strips of stainless steel, which to this day gleam like medieval knights in shining armour.

Modestly referred to as 'the eighth wonder of the world', the Thames Barrier will protect London for at least another 30 years, taking a high estimate of rising sea levels. However, if there were a concerted international response to reduce the man-made causes of global warming, perhaps it would remain effective for even longer.

ADDRESS Unity Way, London SE18 [3B 82]
ENGINEER Rendel, Palmer & Tritton
CONTRACT VALUE approximately £500 million
BR Charlton
ACCESS telephone 0181–854 1373 for Visitors' Centre opening hours and boat cruises

**GLC Department of Architecture 1984**

**Docklands**

**GLC Department of Architecture 1984**

# Beckton Extension
### Docklands Light Railway

Ten new stations have sprung up along an 8-kilometre stretch of land alongside Victoria Dock Road and the Royal Albert Dock Spine Road, extending the Docklands Light Railway to Beckton. Each uses a standard kit, designed to be both unified and flexible: to be identifiable as a route but able to accommodate different site conditions and station types including viaduct stations, island stations, stations built in the middle of roundabouts and the terminus. Staircases, lighting, canopies and lifts have been created on a modular system. Island stations (such as Prince Regent) and viaduct stations (such as Royal Albert) have cantilevered canopies supported by two sets of columns. A row of curved mullions extends from the main columns, spanning the tracks and then wrapped in a toughened glass skin. Electrical cabling is contained within the main columns. Lifts – clad in red vitreous enamel panels – are the only coloured element (all other steelwork blends into the silvery-grey docklandscape), punctured by portholes on each level and glazed on the top to emit a beacon light at night.

The one fundamental flaw in the scheme was the primary consideration for the design of the whole project. Cost-cutting disguised as the Docklands Light Railway 'streamlined service of the future' means that the stations are unmanned – can a light, transparent structure alone accommodate all the safety requirements of passengers?

**Docklands**

CLIENTS London Docklands Development Corporation, Docklands Light Railway
STRUCTURAL ENGINEER The Maunsell Group
CONTRACT VALUE £280 million
ACCESS open during train-timetable hours

**Ahrends Burton & Koralek 1994**

**Ahrends Burton & Koralek 1994**

# Floating Bridge

A tiny creature in the vast urban planes that are Docklands, the floating bridge provides a not as yet absolutely necessary link between Canary Wharf and an expansive, blustery-on-the-calmest-of-days promenade that stretches out in front of some derelict nineteenth-century warehouses on West India Quay (presently under development) – a bridge from nowhere to nowhere. Actually, it is a footbridge: a lime-green, low, squat structure hovering on large padded feet like a waterboatman on a dockland millpond. Its ribbed sides bulge out as if flexed for a leap across to the next quay, with light-emitting handrails to show the way, rather like under-car lighting on a souped-up Ford Fiesta. Curiously, the architect states that 'colour is central to the concept' rather than the conveyance of pedestrians from one side of the water to the other. It nevertheless performs the latter task adequately enough without rising to the vertical challenge of its surroundings. However, if raised above the level of the DLR track entering Canary Wharf it may have afforded an unobstructed view eastwards of the Millennium Dome (see page 342).

ADDRESS north side of West India Quay, London E14 [1C 80]
CLIENT London Docklands Development Corporation
STRUCTURAL ENGINEER Anthony Hunt Associates
SIZE 85-metre span
DOCKLANDS LIGHT RAILWAY Canary Wharf, West India Quay
ACCESS open

**Future Systems 1994**

**Future Systems 1994**

# Limehouse Youth Club

The clients required a well-defended building with a high level of security. At the same time, the clubhouse was to be a focus for the community and therefore had to be easily accessible. The architects arrived at a simple basilica plan, with a central main space flanked by vaulted aisles containing teaching rooms and services. The entrance lobby includes stairs (clearly marked by the protruding glass-block tower) to offices at first-floor level. The apse end, with its ungainly truncated cedar tower that punctures the roof line, was a later addition. The building had to create revenue to maintain it after completion so a 10-metre-high climbing wall (to be hired out to clubs) was added to form one end of the hall. The perimeter is a windowless brickwork base. Natural light is admitted to the aisles through the sides of the shallow-vaulted, millfinished-aluminium-covered roof, which creates a scalloped skirt around the light steel and glass upper storey, which is clad in soft cedar boarding. Natural light enters the central main hall through clerestory windows. Galvanised-metal windows, unpainted brickwork inside and fairfaced concrete columns give the building a tough, durable feel.

The clubhouse maintains the characteristics of the glorified prefab shed. An asset to the community, it sets a standard for future buildings of this type.

ADDRESS Limehouse Causeway, London E14 [7B 64]
CLIENT London Docklands Development Corporation, London Borough of Tower Hamlets, Limehouse Youth Club Support Group
STRUCTURAL ENGINEER TZG Partnership
CONTRACT VALUE £1.1 million SIZE 9000 square metres
DOCKLANDS LIGHT RAILWAY Westferry
ACCESS limited

**Docklands**

**Michael Squire Associates 1995**

**Michael Squire Associates 1995**

# South Dock Footbridge
## Canary Wharf

The brief called for two bridges, the first to span the docks in their present state between the South Quay (Canary Wharf) and Heron Quay. A future phase of development has designated parts of these docks to be in-filled for more building, and another bridge will be required to span a narrower dock. The brief required that the same bridge be used for the two phases. Wilkinson's s-shaped footbridge is constructed in two halves: the Heron Quay side is fixed while the other side swings open around its mast to allow boats to pass. The fixed half can be dismantled and re-erected; the rotating half will remain to be realigned with the new quayside.

The bridge is designed as a cable-stayed structure with two 30-metre inclined steel masts bearing on to piled foundations. A stainless-steel perforated screen forms a balustrade as protection from the prevailing east wind, with a simple aluminium handrail on the other side. The concrete-filled tubular-steel support beam (the one that looks like a sewage pipe) wrapped into the concave side of the bridge is added to balance the asymmetrical lengths of the rotating section. At present the bridge is employed in its phase-one state. The elegance of the intention is obscured by the weight of the engineering challenge. The leaning masts seem to strain under their own weight, let alone that of the footbridge. It remains to be seen how it will adapt to its future incarnation.

ADDRESS south side of West India Docks, London E14 [1C 80]
CLIENT London Docklands Development Corporation
STRUCTURAL ENGINEER Jan Bobrowski & Partners
SIZE 180-metre span
DOCKLANDS LIGHT RAILWAY Canary Wharf, Heron Quays
ACCESS open

**Docklands**

**Chris Wilkinson Architects 1997**

# Millennial sites

# Jubilee Line Extension

In 1993 the chairman of London Transport, Sir Wilfred Newton, invited Roland Paoletti to head a team which would establish – very quickly – a Jubilee Line Extension (JLE) for the London Underground. Paoletti, having worked for the previous 15 years on the new metro system in Hong Kong, knew immediately how he would approach the scheme and which architects he would commission to design the six new stations and remodel and modernise another five. Architects were chosen for their ability to design from first principles, hence the decision to employ mainly younger practices with little or no experience in this field but who showed engineering to be fundamental to their architecture. The use of different architects for each site reinforced the notion of an extension – that is, the task was not to design an entirely new transport system that would be a model for future lines but to celebrate the existing system and its expansion. And as each site presented different conditions and requirements, employing different teams ensured that the architects would define each task anew.

When it opens (spring 1999 is the current target) the JLE will provide a new underground link between central London and the east via the south side of the river and Docklands, with the intention of stimulating the regeneration of these areas. It has been 50 years in the planning, and the history of the transport studies that underly the various routes considered is a book in itself: *Extending the Jubilee Line; The Planning Story* by Jon Willis. At the time of writing many of the stations were nearly complete but there were no working escalators or lifts. So at this stage I cannot assess the architectural merits of each station, but perhaps more appropriately will explain the overall strategy and basic construction of the most important addition to the London Underground (LU) network in 25 years.

**Various architects spring 1999**

**Ian Ritchie Architects**

The route was decided by LU in 1990, and following Paoletti's appointment in 1993 the commissioned architects had just two years to complete their designs. The only givens were the widths of the platforms and tracks. The first principles for the design of each station, as laid out by Paoletti, were driven by what he sees as the current pitiful state of LU (he does not accept the argument that no money equals poor quality) and inspired by his own background in structural architecture (he is a former pupil of Pier Luigi Nervi). The design priorities included generous and easily understood space with as much daylight as possible to generate a sense of ease rather than a labyrinthine effect; clear and direct passenger routing; escalators in a minimum of banks of three; plenty of lifts (there are 118 along the extension – double the number in the entire LU); abundant protected escape routes; and platform-edge glazed screens (the first in the UK) at stations between Westminster and North Greenwich.

Given the vastness of the project and the fact that the architects were employed on design-and-build contracts (handing over the supervision of construction and finishes to separate teams of civil engineers at each site), Paoletti encouraged them to produce simple raw spaces and structures without elaborate finishes (there was no remit, budgetary or otherwise, to design 'posh' stations). The principles of stage lighting are employed to manipulate scale and create atmosphere: house lighting throughout, with spotlights on specific features and a mixture of spot and scenery lighting for maximum dramatic effect. Prioritising the idea that the stations should perform their function spatially, and not ashamed to say they may appear a little rough and ready, Paoletti quotes Louis Khan: 'The right thing done badly is better than the wrong thing done well.'

Three methods of construction were used to build the stations and two main tunnelling systems dealt with specific ground conditions. New plat-

**Ian Ritchie Architects**

forms and tunnels at **London Bridge** (Jubilee Line Extension Architects & Weston Williamson), already London's busiest interchange, and **Waterloo** (Jubilee Line Extension Architects), an international interchange, called for underground mining and excavation of London clay. Huge caverns were created using the New Austrian Tunnelling Method (NATM), which as it digs sprays a thin layer of quick-setting concrete to the walls, to be reinforced later with steel mesh and more concrete.

**Westminster, Southwark** and **Bermondsey** are combined open-cut boxes (like open-heart surgery) with mined tunnels to platform levels. Westminster (Michael Hopkins and Partners) was the most complex and restricted work site on a very deep section of the line. An entirely-new station box replaces the old Victorian structure, revealing an open-plan escalator well combined with the foundations for the new parliamentary building which will eventually be above the station – all constructed within close proximity to key landmark buildings while keeping existing lines operational. The construction of a new interchange with mainline services at Waterloo East at Southwark (McCormac Jamieson Prichard; see page 329) was dominated by a fragile mainline viaduct nearby. All earth and building movements were monitored by computer and any slumps compensated for by compensation grouting (a method of shoring up weak areas of earth by injecting strands of grout into the ground to build up a cobweb of reinforcement that was used throughout the project, particularly in built-up areas). The rounded entrance and ticket hall are formed from smooth concrete beams that create a lantern of natural light above the platforms. At Bermondsey (Ian Ritchie Architects; see page 327) natural light is exploited by providing a translucent roof like a glass lid over the main concourse. This is the area's first Underground station: 4.35-metre-diameter running tunnels were driven from London Bridge

**Chris Wilkinson Architects**

to Canada Water, enlarged to 7 metres for the 100-metre-long platform tunnels inside the station.

**Canada Water**, **Canary Wharf** and **North Greenwich** are large, open-box, cut-and-cover structures with the 140-metre-long platforms built into the bottom levels. The only visible signs of a station at Canada Water (Jubilee Line Extension Architects) are a shallow glass drum and a triangular ventilation shaft; the rest of its mass (comparable in size to St Paul's Cathedral) is 23 metres below the surface. The open box at Canary Wharf (Sir Norman Foster & Partners; see page 333) measures 280 metres long and 32 metres wide (large enough to encase the Canary Wharf tower on its side) and is 24 metres below pavement level. The only visible signs of the station on the surface are two shallow stingray-shaped glass canopies identifying entrances at each end of the landscaped garden that forms the roof for the exposed-concrete cavern below. 160,000 tonnes of water were drained from West India Quay to create a dry bed, with 'de-watering' wells driven 55 metres into the underlying chalk to keep the dock from flooding during construction. North Greenwich (Alsop Lyall & Störmer & Jubilee Line Extension Architects; see page 335), the world's largest Underground station, is 405 metres long and 32 metres wide, and required the removal of 300,000 cubic metres of spoil (soil and rubble). The main concourse, shaped like the underbelly of a whale, is suspended above the tracks with views down to platforms on either side. The roof is supported by 21 pairs of 13-metre-high sloping columns. The station's structure is held down simply by its own weight. Surfaces are treated with various materials all saturated with underwater deep blue.

**Canning Town**, **West Ham** and **Stratford** are all multi-level stations. At Canning Town (Troughton McAslan; see page 337) an underground concourse supports six tracks and three platforms. The Docklands Light

**Various architects**

**Sir Norman Foster & Partners**

Railway tracks are elevated above the Jubilee Line and the below-ground platforms link to the ground-level North London Line and new bus station. At West Ham (Van Heyningen & Haward) an existing station has been completely redesigned. A low, utilitarian red- and glass-brick building bridges three railway lines and a major road. Stratford (see page 331), the grand terminus, is the work of two different teams. Troughton McAslan designed the platforms and accommodation building; the 'breaking wave' that is the distinctive concourse building is by Chris Wilkinson Architects. The station is at surface level and the concourse building provides an interchange between five different railway lines and the bus station. The sweep of the curved roof breaks over a sloping glass screen wall that faces towards the town centre and the Jubilee Line; all other sides of the building are also glazed to provide clear views out to other lines and to maximise daylight and natural ventilation. A mezzanine level provides direct access to the mainline railway with the lower-level concourse serving the underground lines. Sheltered seating areas made of ceramic-faced blockwork and covered by wing-shaped aluminium canopies are located along the new platforms.

A project of this size inevitably encounters practical problems. One of the biggest was the collapse of the sprayed-concrete NATM tunnel at Heathrow, which (although not directly associated with the Jubilee Line Extension) halted work until the system could be proved safe. The scale and complexity of construction, particularly in areas where Underground services had to be maintained, led to overspending. In parallel with this are the scale and complexity of co-ordinating separate civil-, mechanical- and electrical-engineering contracts at each site, with up to 15 different contractors working simultaneously. A crucial question is whether

**Various architects**

**Millennial sites**

**Alsop & Störmer**

London Transport will maintain the stations (which have been designed to last 100 years) to a high standard.

What long-term effect will the JLE have on the map of central London? A small research team at the University of Westminster is currently devising a data-collection programme to provide future transport planners with information about the impact of such proposals. The benefits of the link will inform future decisions about the proposed Crossrail route from Stratford to Paddington (*en route* for Heathrow), a Chelsea/ Hackney Line and the Thames Gateway Metro – all of which would not only significantly reduce road traffic and make for a more efficient transport system, but could provide architects with the challenge of creating another kind of architecture for the city.

**Millennial sites**

ACCESS due to open to fare-paying passengers in autumn 1999, but the completion date remains interestingly uncertain at the time of going to press

**Various architects**

**Troughton McAslan**

# Millennium Projects

A few projects currently on site and due for completion in time for the millennium are:

The redevelopment of the **Royal Opera House** in Bow Street, WC2 by Dixon Jones and BDP (see page 339). As yet the building schedule seems unhampered by the Royal Opera's catastrophic internal political and administrative wranglings which have come under the scrutiny of a government Select Committee. The project involves the remodelling of a building designed by E M Barry in 1858 with a frieze by John Flaxman under the portico made in Coade Stone, a highly durable artificial stone developed in the eighteenth century in Lambeth. (The secret of the composition was lost when the factory closed in 1840.) Some small additions were made to the building on to James Street in the early 1980s, but the current scheme extends the theatre itself (primarily the backstage facilities) further south to meet Russell Street. Let's hope that once work is complete there will be a secure (and inspired) administration in place to make good use of the facility.

The British Film Institute's **IMAX Cinema** by Avery Associates Architects infills the sunken roundabout on the south side of Waterloo Bridge. The site is close to the South Bank Centre, Waterloo Station and the Jubilee Gardens (site of the Millennium Wheel – see below). One gets the feeling this project is driven simply by the urge to create an instant wow and to cash in on a strategic site. It is surprising that such a supposedly distinguished institution should be funding a gimmick like this while simultaneously withdrawing all funding support from feature-film production in this country – especially as there is already a three-dimensional screen at the Trocadero complex in Piccadilly. I would sooner hop on the

**Dixon Jones and BDP/Avery Associates Architects**

**Dixon Jones and BDP**

Eurostar and go to Bernard Tschumi's Parc de la Villette in Paris, watch the same IMAX movies inside a mirrored geodesic dome, and wander around the most remarkable urban park to be designed this century.

During the 1980s Will Alsop (of Alsop & Störmer) was labelled an *enfant terrible* of British architecture. To date the practice's work has only been built on a large scale and celebrated in Europe (the 'Grand Bleu' city hall in Marseilles and projects in Holland and Germany), so it is with bated breath that we look forward to the **Peckham Library and Media Centre**.

The scheme for the **Tate Gallery of Modern Art** by Swiss architects Herzog & de Meuron (see page 341) involves the restructuring of Bankside Power Station, designed by Sir Giles Gilbert Scott who also designed Battersea Power Station. The building will house the Tate's twentieth-century collection in purpose-built gallery space stacked on top of the original brick structure, with the ground-floor engine rooms creating vast public areas for circulation and large sculpture installations. It remains to be seen what will occur inside the tower. One questions the decision by the Tate to create a gallery exclusively for the display of twentieth-century works, which can only fuel the cynical attitude the British press encourages the nation to adopt towards contemporary art. The beauty of the Tate Gallery on Millbank is that its mixed collection and layout mean that even those visitors interested in only one school of painting cannot fail to encounter works from other periods. However, it seems likely that the enormous building at Bankside will exude a cathedral-like aura and it can only benefit the slowly developing area in which it is located. Approach from the riverside walk or Sumner Street off Southwark Street.

**Alsop & Störmer/Herzog & de Meuron**

**Herzog & de Meuron**

One of the few projects that has not called on lottery or public funds is the **British Airways Millennium Wheel** (funded by the Millennium Wheel Company), designed by David Marks Julia Barfield Architects and engineered by Ove Arup & Partners; see page 343). It is located in Jubilee Gardens on the south bank of the Thames. Although it is designed to remain on the site for only five years, the idea is that the Wheel will act as a magnet to the millions of visitors to London, attracting them from Big Ben across Westminster Bridge to the South Bank. George Washington Gale Ferris Jr designed the first such wheel – which stood at 76 metres high – for the 1893 World's Colombian Exposition in Chicago. The 135-metre-diameter Millennium Wheel will be turned on its rim by two motors on the base boarding-platform. Sixty enclosed 20-seater capsules will carry passengers for a 25-minute 'flight' over the heart of the capital accompanied by a commentary on the major landmark sites encompassed in their view. Solar cells will be incorporated into the capsules to help power ventilation, lighting and communication systems. To ensure stability in high winds, 10-metre-long outriggers tie back to the ground from the centre spindle. Tenuous suggestions have been offered as to the symbolic potency of the wheel, ranging from the 'cycles of life' to the capsules 'reflecting the minutes and seconds of time itself'. The highest observation wheel in the world will be, if nothing else, a shot in the arm for London's tourist industry and a tremendous marketing ploy for its sponsors.

Which leads to the ultimate attraction – or more accurately, what the government prays will be every British family's holiday destination of choice throughout the year 2000 and beyond: the polluted site of a former gas works, or, rather, the **Millennium Dome** (see page 345), located at zero

**David Marks Julia Barfield Architects**

**David Marks Julia Barfield Architects**

degrees longitude and mean time, Greenwich. Designed by Richard Rogers Partnership, the dome is technically a tent (some prefer to call it a 'big top'). Twelve masts are positioned around a 364-metre-diameter base, creating 80,000 square metres of floor area. The 90-metre-high masts, resting on 10-metre-high quadropods, support a grid of cables (using 67 kilometres of cable) which forms the domed cobweb (50 metres high at its apex) to which 150,000 square metres of Teflon-coated glass-fibre fabric adhere to create an enclosure (big enough to house 18,000 double-decker buses). The risk of indoor rain clouds forming if condensation were to build up has been avoided by applying two layers of fabric for insulation. The largest fabric-covered structure of its kind ever made is unfortunately punctured by the ventilation tower for the Blackwall Tunnel, which releases excessive car-exhaust fumes from the tunnel into the surrounding atmosphere. The cost of the building itself is estimated at £54 million while the cost of cleaning up and developing the immediate surroundings is considerably higher at a total of £750 million (provided by the lottery and private business). The area will be serviced by the new North Greenwich Underground station on the Jubilee Line Extension designed by Alsop & Störmer (see page 332), though there are concerns that this alone will be unable to cope with the numbers of visitors that will/must arrive each day.

The Dome was the brainchild of the Conservative government in 1994. Despite serious protests from the Opposition at the time as to the symbolism of the Dome as a celebration of private enterprise, a change of government in 1997 saw it adopted as a New Labour monument. The huge controversy over what will fill it is in design terms its most inelegant feature and politically the most revealing aspect of the project. The New Millennium Experience Company (a management body rather than a

**Richard Rogers Partnership**

**Richard Rogers Partnership**

creative one) revealed proposals in 1998 for a series of separate themed exhibitions to be designed by smaller architectural practices, the focus of which will be the 'Body Zone', a 50-metre-high androgenous figure that can be explored internally via any orifice. But the most elegant and lasting feature of the Dome is that the entire structure (all 1800 tonnes of it) weighs less than the air inside. This fact alone would be enough of an attraction to lure the most stubborn of sceptics to experience the phenomenon without the need for sub-Disneyesque distractions.

ADDRESSES Millennium Dome: E14, exit off A102 Blackwall Tunnel Approach, (North Greenwich station); British Airways Millennium Wheel: Jubilee Gardens, South Bank SE1 (Waterloo station); Tate Gallery of Modern Art: Bankside, SE1 (Southwark station); Royal Opera House, Bow Street, WC2 (Covent Garden station); BFI IMAX Cinema: centre of the roundabout at Tenison Way, SE1 (Waterloo station); Peckham Library and Media Centre: 126–130 Peckham Hill Street, SE15

**Richard Rogers Partnership**

**Richard Rogers Partnership**

# Index

London: a guide to recent architecture

London: a guide to recent architecture

London: a guide to recent architecture

London: a guide to recent architecture

PHOTOGRAPHS by Keith Collie except:
pages 119, 121 Heike Löwenstein
pages 149, 151 Jocelyne van den Bossche
page 209 Charlotte Wood
The drawing on page 207 is reproduced
by permission of Allies & Morrison
The CAD image on page 327 is reproduced
by permission of Ian Ritchie Architects
The drawing on page 339 is reproduced
by permission of Dixon Jones
The image on page 343 is reproduced by
permission of Nick Wood/David Marks
Julia Barfield Limited